WORD AND WORLD

By the same author

PRAYERS OF THE NEW TESTAMENT
FIVE MAKERS OF THE NEW TESTAMENT
SINEWS OF FAITH
STEWARDS OF GRACE

WORD AND WORLD

by
DONALD COGGAN

Archbishop of York

HODDER AND STOUGHTON
LONDON SYDNEY AUCKLAND TORONTO

The extract from *The History of the British and Foreign Bible Society, 1905–1954* by J. M. Roe on pp. 88–89 appears by permission of the British and Foreign Bible Society.

For

OLIVIER BÉGUIN

who since 1949 has been the
indefatigable General Secretary
of the United Bible Societies

and

to the memory of

FRANK LAUBACH

apostle of literacy

and of

EIVIND JOSEF BERGGRAV

Bishop of Oslo

a builder of the World Council of Churches,
first President of the United Bible Societies,
and 'a man of the Bible'.

Oure fadir that art in heuenes,
Halwid bi thi name;
Thi kyngdom cumme to;
Be thi wille don as in heuen and in erthe;
Gif to vs this day oure breed ouer other substaunce;
And forgeue to vs oure dettis,
As we forgeue to oure dettours;
And leede vs nat in to temptacioun,
But delyuere vs fro yvel.
Amen.

Wycliffite Version, 1382.

Preface

Just before his book *Church and Gnosis* appeared in 1932, the late Professor F. C. Burkitt impressed upon me the importance of choosing short titles for the books one wrote. He was pleased with the title *Church and Gnosis*. I have borne his admonition in mind. Perhaps the title is the best part of this book—*Word and World*. *Word* here means more than the Bible. It stands for that primarily, but also for that vast body of literature which expounds the Bible and relates its principles to life. And *World*—well, that means what it says, our present-day exhilarating, frightened, tragic, glorious world, the world God made and loves, the world for which Christ died.

The area covered is thus a large one. The story of the growth of the English Bible alone is a long, deeply interesting and complex one, as the following chapters indicate—and they give but an outline. But when we reach out beyond this—as this book attempts to do—to the whole field of Christian literature and to the place of its dissemination in the strategy of the Church, we are embarking on a task which would call for an author far more learned and knowledgeable than the present one, and for a row of volumes rather than this modest one. However, there is something to be said for a bird's-eye view of the story of the past, for an assessment of the problems and opportunities of the present, and for a summons to action in the future.

I must express my gratitude to many:

To the trustees of the Duff Missionary Lectureship Trust who have done me the honour of asking me to deliver the lectures which, in an extended form, make up the substance of this book. Having read and profited from William Paton's book *Alexander Duff— Pioneer of Missionary Education* (S.C.M.P., 1923), I dare to believe that the man in whose memory these lectures are given would

7

approve of the general theme of this book and appreciate the urgency of its main thesis.

To Mrs. Stayt, of Fonderling, Underberg, Natal, and the Bishop of George and Mrs. Patrick Barron, in whose homes I was able to get the quiet necessary to make a substantial start on the writing of this book.

To my wife, for her encouragement, and for her patience in making the indexes.

To my secretary, Miss Mavis Bulmer, for her skill in deciphering my manuscript and in typing and retyping the chapters.

To my Lay Chaplain, Mr. D. A. C. Blunt, for his kindness in reading the proofs.

To Messrs. Longmans, Green and Co., for permission to include in Chapter 5 some material from my booklet *The English Bible* in their *Writers and their Work Series* No. 154 (1963, reprinted 1968; published by Longmans Group Limited for the British Council).

Alexander Duff was a man with a passion—to bring education, based firmly on Christian foundations, to the peoples of India. This book is written in the conviction that the main hope of our world, torn by rival ideologies and perplexed by new knowledge, is to be found in the dissemination and the application of the principles of life which are to be found in Christ crucified and risen, which are recorded in the Christian Scriptures, and which must be enunciated, expounded, applied in literature of all languages and at all levels, and by use of the mass media which are increasingly becoming the main means of communication between nations and individuals.

Contents

Chapter		page
1	'The Greatest Drama Ever Staged'	13
2	Early Christian Writing	23
3	'Every Man in his Own Language'	31
4	'Deathless Minds which Leave . . . a Path of Light'	41
5	A Century of Advance (1870–1970)	67
6	'Into All the World'	81
7	With Note and Comment	99
8	The Task Today and Tomorrow	110
9	'In Full Assurance of Faith'	129
	Epilogue	146
	Appendix I: Member Societies and Associate Members of the United Bible Societies	149
	Appendix II: 'A Solemn and Urgent Appeal'	150
	Index to Biblical References	153
	General Index	155

Illustrations

between pages 80 and 81

Papyrus in possession of the John Rylands Library

William Tyndale[1]

The directors of the New English Bible[2]

The last meeting of the Joint Committee of sponsoring Churches before publication of the complete New English Bible[2]

A group of students at the Africa Literature Centre

A stop-over for the Bookvan at a hospital in Zambia

The Dag Hammarskjöld Memorial Library at the Mindolo Ecumenical Centre, Zambia

Printing *New Day*

Christian books find interested readers amongst Hong Kong schoolboys

KEY TO ACKNOWLEDGEMENTS

[1] Lutterworth Press

[2] London News Agency Photos Ltd

1

'The Greatest Drama Ever Staged'

'The greatest drama ever staged'. It was natural that Dorothy Sayers should describe the Christ-event in this way, for she was a dramatist and playwright, as well as a writer of thrillers.

Something happened when Christ was born and lived and died and rose. 'If this is dull,' she wrote, 'then what, in Heaven's name, is worthy to be called exciting?'[1] Something inexpressibly wonderful happened. Precisely so. And yet it had to be expressed, and re-expressed, and expressed again for succeeding generations to hear and grasp and appropriate.

This 'expressing' is one of the two main reasons for the existence of the Christian Church. If its first raison-d'être is the worship of Almighty God, its second is the expression of those events which constitute the Christian gospel, the shewing forth of 'the praises of him who hath called you out of darkness into his marvellous light'.[2]

Christianity is an historical religion. It is not primarily a code of ethics, though it is a deeply ethical religion. T. W. Manson used to say that Christ gave his followers direction rather than directions, thus treating them as adults and making demands on their intelligence. And Kirkegaard never tired of insisting that ethics only make us aware of our failures, whereas what we need is new life, a rebirth. Nor is Christianity primarily a new philosophy, though many of the greatest philosophers have found their highest inspiration in it. No: when we say that Christianity is an historical religion we mean that its roots go down firmly into the soil of a particular land at a particular period in the long and troubled evolution of our race.

[1] D. Sayers, *The Greatest Drama Ever Staged* (Hodder and Stoughton, 1938), p. 14
[2] 1 Pet. 2:9

The preparation for the coming of the Christ was long. The beginnings are hidden in the mists of antiquity. 'In fragmentary and varied fashion through the prophets,' God spoke.[3] But speak he did, making himself known as Yahweh, the self-disclosing God—'I am that I am', or 'I will be what I will be', or 'I will become what I will become',[4] the God who, as Péguy says, 'is both youthful and eternal'. The ancient ideas of taboo and of sacrificial ritual may seem very remote from the thought-forms of the men of a sophisticated and technological generation. But at least we can see how the holiness, the 'otherness', of God revealed itself to the Hebrew people, who sensed his majesty in distant star and awful thunder and frightening storm. 'Put off thy shoes from off thy feet, for the place whereon thou standest is holy ground!'[5] Moses learnt his lesson, as others were to learn it too. And together with the 'otherness' of God, they learnt perhaps more slowly and painfully (yet also joyfully) of the faithfulness of God, his utter reliability. He was the God who would enter into a covenant relationship with his people and would remain true to that agreement however great the strain might be which was imposed by man's faithlessness. His 'justice' was not some abstract quality or virtue which could be posited of him in some remote philosophical sense. On the contrary, it was a factor, a force, in history, in the affairs of men and of nations, which had to be reckoned with. In the later prophets, Yahweh was envisaged as one who moved earth's rulers according to his sovereign will—not merely a David or a Solomon, but a Cyrus and a Nebuchadnezzar.[6] They, little as they knew it, were to be his agents in the fulfilling of a purpose which reached out far beyond the limits of Israel to the remote corners of the earth. The King who reigned in righteousness was at once the God of holiness and faithfulness and the God of love. His love was such that it could only be spoken of in parental terms—'like as a father pitieth his children, so the Lord pitieth them that fear him'.[7] 'Can a woman forget her sucking child, that she should not have compassion on

[3] Heb. 1:1 N.E.B.
[4] Exod. 3:14
[5] Exod. 3:5
[6] Isa. 44:28 and 45:1; Jer. 43:10
[7] Ps. 103:13

the son of her womb? Yea, they may forget, yet will I not forget thee.'[8]

Slowly, painfully slowly, the nature of such a God was glimpsed. The vision had its difficulties, and often they seemed terrifyingly large. *If* God was like what the prophets said he was, then why . . .? Why the prosperity of the wicked? Why the defeat of the good? Why the extraordinary story of man's inhumanity to man? Why human suffering? Why premature death? Why . . .? The working out of a theodicy, a justification of the character of God and of his ways with men, was not easy. The book of Job, to take but one instance (albeit the outstanding one) from the pages of the Old Testament, is the story, couched in dramatic form, of the protest of a good man against the injustices of life and of the (to him) inexplicable ways of God with men. 'Ye have heard of the patience of Job'[9] is a patently false translation; Job is the most impatient figure in the Old Testament, his book being one long protest against the injustice of life. 'You have all heard how Job stood firm';[10] that is a very different matter, and true to the facts of the drama. The very considerable body of apocalyptic literature, of which the main example in the Old Testament is the book of Daniel, is an attempt to wrestle with, and perhaps give birth to, some solution of this problem. As one reads this strange genre of writing, one can envisage the writers almost like bears caught in a tangle of netting. As one tries to get to grips with their complicated imagery of beasts and strange creatures half-human half-demonic, one can begin to see the emergence of a doctrine, often crude, of an after-life on which it was possible for later thinkers and preachers—and not least our Lord himself—to build. They were great pioneers in the complex task of constructing a theodicy.

Then he came. The exact date of the birth of Jesus of Nazareth, as of his death, is unknown. But the evangelists place it firmly in the setting, historical and geographical, of Palestine when Tiberius was Emperor. If St. Luke had an eye on the world situation and on the

[8] Isa. 49:15
[9] Jas. 5:11
[10] N.E.B.

Roman Government,[11] St. Matthew traced the genealogy of Jesus through the deportation back to David and back again to Abraham.[12] 'So the drama of the ages is played out on the stage of a small province of the Roman Empire in the first century of our era. We see the clash of forces, we hear the battle of words. The ultimate result on the human plane is never really in doubt. Yet the central figure goes forward, not without struggle, but with the assurance that He is fulfilling a Divine purpose however mysterious it may seem to human eyes.'[13]

The time was ripe. In Pauline language 'the fullness of time' had come when God sent forth his Son.[14] The God of history is never too early, never tardy, in the timing of his mighty acts. A great peace wrapped the Graeco-Roman world—Pliny the Elder called it in a memorable phrase, *immensa Romanae pacis majestas*.[15] True, there were eruptions from time to time, but they were held in check by the force of Roman rule and arms, exercised sometimes roughly, sometimes with a crude charity. Without such a peace, it would have been difficult for the Christian message to run its course freely. As it was,

> No war, no battle's sound
> Was heard the world around:
> The idle spear and shield were high up hung,
> The hookéd chariot stood
> Unstain'd with hostile blood,
> The trumpet spake not to the arméd throng
> And kings sat still with awful eye
> As if they surely knew their sov'reign Lord was by.[16]

Further, there was a common language used and understood in most parts of the far-flung Empire. Greek, most delicate and most

[11] Luke 3:1
[12] Matt. 1:1–17
[13] F. W. Dillistone, *The Christian Understanding of Atonement* (Nisbet, 1968), p. 138
[14] Gal. 4:4
[15] Pliny, *Natural History*, XXVII, 1, iii
[16] Milton, *On the Morning of Christ's Nativity*

expressive of all languages, was the lingua franca of the Graeco-Roman world. When St. Paul wrote his letter to the Romans (to take but one example), he wrote it not in Latin but in Greek. So the Gospel, once it leapt out of the confines of Palestine, could be understood well-nigh universally without the necessity, *at the start*, for a battle on the part of the preachers with the curse of Babel. Just as the network of Roman roads made a highway for the Gospel, so the fact of an almost universally understood language prepared the way for the messengers of peace.

Two other factors may be mentioned to illustrate what is meant by 'the fullness of time'. There was a certain weariness, a *taedium vitae*, in society. Men were tired of 'gods many and lords many',[17] of the ancient myths and of unsatisfying philosophies. The 'first fine careless rapture' of the great classical period was over. Where could truth and goodness and beauty be found? Where could life in its fullness be discovered? And within Israel itself, there was much religion but a terrible lack of prophecy in the true sense of the word. That silence is poignantly hinted at by the writer of 1 Maccabees,[18] who describes how Judas Maccabaeus and his brothers found the altar at Jerusalem desecrated, pulled it down, 'and stored away the stones in a fitting place on the temple hill, *until a prophet should arise* who could be consulted about them'. It was time for him to come whose purpose in coming was 'that men may have life, and have it in all its fullness'.[19] And when he came, it was like the coming of a gale of fresh air into an atmosphere grown stale and foetid.

The second factor was the presence of the Septuagint, the translation into Greek of what we now call the Old Testament. Tradition maintains that Ptolemy Philadelphus (285–246 B.C.) wanted a translated copy of the Hebrew Law for his Library at Alexandria and engaged seventy-two translators to do the work. The story grew with the passing of the years, and we need not believe it all. What seems clear, however, is that several scholars did the work, that it extended over a considerable period of time, and that it was virtually complete at any rate by 132 B.C.

---

[17] 1 Cor. 8:5
[18] 1 Macc. 4:46 N.E.B.
[19] John 10:10 N.E.B.

The immense influence of the Septuagint on the writers of the New Testament is recognised by all biblical scholars. What is more important for our purpose is the fact that long before Jesus Christ was born, long before the New Testament came to be written, the Septuagint had been doing its work, had indeed itself become a vital part of the *preparatio evangelica*.

The synagogue has been rightly called 'the first apostle to the Gentiles'. Wherever there was a community among which twelve adult males could be numbered, there it was permitted to found a synagogue. These widely-scattered Jewish communities became the centres, not only of worship, education and law for the Jews of the *Diaspora*, but also centres of great interest for those Gentiles—and they were many—who were drawn to what they had seen and heard of Jewish faith and practice. Many of the finest Gentile minds were tiring of the tenets of polytheism. They were drawn to a mono-theistic religion which could speak of a God who loved his people and of the possibility of men loving God, a religion which was becoming more missionary in its outlook as the universalism of some of the prophets came to be understood. If circumcision proved a stumbling-block to their becoming fully committed adherents of Judaism, then they would have to be content to be among that big class of people which the New Testament refers to as 'godfearers', men on the fringe of the synagogue, learning of Yahweh, and somewhat wistfully wanting to follow him. But of what use would the synagogue have been to such men if the Scrip-tures which were read so regularly in them had been available only in Hebrew? Knowledge of that language, and of its kindred tongue Aramaic, was the almost exclusive possession of those who lived in Palestine and of those devout Jews who travelled abroad on their lawful occasions. It was not—and it never became—the lingua franca of the Graeco-Roman world. That was reserved for Greek, perhaps the most beautiful, accurate, and expressive language of all the languages of mankind.

It is the fact of synagogues scattered throughout the world, combined with the fact that these synagogues were 'nurseries of Mosaism' in which the Hebrew Scriptures were available *in Greek* to a wide circle of hearers and readers, that makes it possible for us to think of these synagogues as the first apostles to the Gentiles, and of the buildings and the book as constituting a very powerful *preparatio evangelica*.

All was ready, then, for the coming of the Word made flesh. The setting for the great divine drama was complete. So God could speak to men as he had never done before. Goethe, centuries later, said, 'The highest cannot be spoken: it can only be acted'. Pavlova, in our own day, in reply to a question as to what she meant by a dance which she had just performed, replied, 'Do you think I would have *danced* it if I could have *said* it?' So Jesus did not merely speak to men the word of God as the prophets had done before him. He *was* the Word of God. He acted out the mind and heart and will of God. 'He came to dwell among us', thus anchoring the Eternal in human history. Leslie Davison has put it well: 'In Jesus is disclosed as much of God as man can know in this phase of existence.'[20] That—and much more—is what St. John meant when he spoke, in the prologue to his Gospel, of Jesus as the Word of God, full of grace and truth.

There, in Galilee, in Samaria, in Judaea, something happened, inexpressibly wonderful, but demanding expression. *How was it to be expressed*, when the bodily presence of Jesus was withdrawn and a handful of very ordinary men and women were the only visible results of the life and ministry and passion of the Son of Man? There were three main ways.

The *first* was the way of the *sacraments*. Baptism and the Eucharist were designed to be *verba visibilia*, words made visible to the eye, expressions of the love and grace of God which could be sensibly experienced. Through them the love of God could invade the whole of a man, moving him, cleansing him, re-vivifying him, strengthening him. 'Every time you eat this bread and drink the cup, you proclaim the death of the Lord, until he comes.'[21] The word 'proclaim' ('ye do shew', A.V.) is the ordinary word used by St. Paul and in the Acts of *declaring* 'the attested truth of God',[22] of

[20] L. Davison, *Sender and Sent: A Study in Mission* (Epworth Press, 1969), p. 33
[21] 1 Cor. 11:26 N.E.B.
[22] 1 Cor. 2:1 N.E.B.

preaching the Gospel.[23] This is just what sacraments do. They declare. They preach. Through eye, through the senses, they convey to men the manifold grace of God. Then, as the Church spread throughout the world and countless communities became obedient to the word of the Gospel, the sacraments proved to be a divinely adhesive force. 'One Lord, one faith, one baptism.'[24] The worldwide Church began to experience the truth expressed in the words *oceanis divisi, sacramentis conjuncti*, men divided by oceans found themselves united by the sacraments. So the inexpressible was expressed; the love of God, made known in his incarnate Son, was unceasingly declared, for not a day has passed since the ascension of our Lord, when the community of the baptised has not proclaimed, declared, preached his death in the sacrament of the Eucharist 'till he come'.

The *second* way was the way of the *word*. It began completely informally. The joy of the new life which the early disciples experienced in Christ had to find expression in words, faltering often enough, desperately inadequate to express the inexpressible love of God. One told another—here a soldier of Caesar who was also a soldier of the Cross told his fellow-soldier of a service which was perfect freedom; there a housewife told her friend of one who lifted burdens and carried sorrows. They 'gossiped the Gospel', and so it spread like wildfire. There was something infectious, contagious, in the new-found faith. Christianity was caught before it was formally taught. One told another; it was as simple as that. It was the way of the spoken word.

But there was also the more formal way of the preaching of the word. The reader has not to go far into the Acts of the Apostles before he finds the leaders of the Church busy with the task of preaching the faith to the multitudes who were prepared to listen. The content of the apostolic preaching, as it is summarised in the Acts, makes a fascinating study.[25] The various words used to describe the preaching have as their objects 'the word of the Lord'

[23] 1 Cor. 9:14
[24] Eph. 4:5
[25] See especially C. H. Dodd, *The Apostolic Preaching and its Developments* (Hodder and Stoughton, 1936), and note also my *The Ministry of the Word* (Lutterworth, revised edn. 1964), especially chapter 5.

(or 'of God'), and, very frequently, 'Jesus', or 'Jesus Christ', or 'Jesus, the Son of God', and again such phrases as 'the Reign of God', or 'peace by Jesus Christ', or 'the forgiveness of sins', this latter being closely linked with the Person and work of our Lord. It is crystal clear that the centre and focus of the preaching of the early Church was Christ crucified, risen, and exalted. With their Scriptures 'come alive' in the recent events which they had shared in with Jesus of Nazareth, the preaching of the apostles was a good example of the definition of Christian preaching given by Bernard Lord Manning: 'A manifestation of the Incarnate Word, from the Written Word, by the spoken word.'[26]

The *third* way was the way of the Spirit-controlled life. Here was evidence irrefutable. When men saw their fellow-men with minds re-made and their whole nature transformed,[27] they were confronted by flesh and blood instances of the love of God at work. These Christians were men with a new motivation. They were quite obviously sons of God, for they were moved by the Spirit of God,[28] just as God's incarnate Son had been baptised, empowered, moved and activated by the Spirit.[29] The Spirit was obviously the source of their life; the Spirit was directing their course.[30] Instead of the behaviour which in the old days belonged to their lower nature, a new harvest, the harvest of a Christ-like character, was being reaped,[31] which itself was an expression of the inexpressible love of God in Christ. Originally 'how these Christians love one another' was said not cynically but in surprise and admiration. As T. R. Glover put it, the early Christians out-lived, out-thought, and out-died their contemporaries, many of them going to their deaths as to a wedding.

St. Luke sums it all up admirably in the second chapter of the Acts—one can sense the freedom and the joy of the new life effervescing, as it were, in the context of sacrament and of word.

[26] Bernard Manning, *A Layman in the Ministry* (Independent Press, 1942), p. 138
[27] Rom. 12:2
[28] Rom. 8:14
[29] Luke 3:22; 4:1, 14, 18
[30] Gal. 5:25
[31] Gal. 5:19–23

'Then those who accepted [Peter's] word were baptised . . . They met constantly to hear the apostles teach, and to share the common life, to break bread, and to pray. A sense of awe was everywhere . . . many marvels and signs were brought about . . . All whose faith had drawn them together held everything in common . . . With one mind they kept up their daily attendance at the temple, and, breaking bread in private houses, shared their meals with unaffected joy, as they praised God and enjoyed the favour of the whole people.'[32]

Such was the way in which the members of the early Church shewed forth the praises of him who had called them out of darkness into his marvellous light.

It was good, wonderfully good. But it was not enough.

[32] Acts 2:41–47 N.E.B.

2

Early Christian Writing

Life is brittle and man's span of years is brief. His transitoriness is a fact with which each individual and each generation has to come to terms. How can continuity be established? How can the next generation be linked with the preceding one without a break or without a disruptive change taking place in what has to be handed on? How can the reliability of tradition be ensured?

The young churches had to face these problems very early in their existence. Jesus died, and rose, and his bodily presence was withdrawn. True, he had promised the gift of the Holy Spirit, his Other Self, who would teach the disciples and bring all things to their remembrance.[1] True, this became a living reality to them. But this was not an easy solution to all the problems that faced them. Indeed, the problems proved more pressing and urgent as year succeeded year. They confidently hoped that, within a brief period, he would return and they would see once again, with their own eyes, the Lord whom they had loved and followed in his earthly ministry. But they were disappointed. He did not come on the clouds of heaven. A major readjustment in their thinking, in their living, and in their planning for the future had to take place.

The first generation began to die off. St. Peter and, very likely, St. Paul were martyred in the persecution under Nero who died in A.D. 68. The apostles scattered and we know little of what happened to them—did St. Thomas reach India? There is a persistent tradition that he did and that he founded the Church there. St. John apparently lived on to a great old age, but it is likely that he was dead by the turn of the century. Jerome tells how, in his old age when he was too weak to speak with his former vigour, John used to be carried to meetings of Christians and to say repeatedly, 'Little

[1] John 14:26

23

children, love one another.'[2] But that generation at last came to an
end, and none was left who had known Jesus in the flesh.

The sacraments remained. The word remained, both in the
informal 'gossiping of the Gospel' and in the more formal preaching of liturgical and evangelistic activity. The evidence of the
Spirit-controlled lives of the faithful remained. But certain questions arose which became more pressing as every year passed. It
was all very well to celebrate the Eucharist every Sunday in, let us
say, Ephesus or Rome or Philippi. But these places were far
removed from Jerusalem where first the Eucharist was instituted.
Distance in geography and distance in time combined to raise
certain questions, not to mention the fact that Jesus talked Aramaic
with his disciples at the Last Supper, while Greek was the language
used in Ephesus and Rome and Philippi. How, then, could one be
sure that there would be a measure of reliability, of accurate continuity, between what happened in Jerusalem that memorable
night and what was happening every week in the little assemblies
scattered throughout the Graeco-Roman world as the missionary
work of the Church extended?

It was all very well to speak of 'preaching the Gospel'. But what
was the Gospel? It was obviously essential to teach the faith to
people who had never seen Jesus or heard his voice or, for that
matter, the voices of his first disciples. And soon it would be
necessary to teach that faith to the children of the first generation
of Christian disciples. But what *was* the faith? What were the facts
about the life and death of Jesus of Nazareth? About his resurrection? What did he teach on matters of crucial moral and ethical
importance? The questions were legion and urgent, and were felt
with peculiar force by those who were the first teachers and
preachers of the word and who first exercised pastoral responsibility
in the churches. Tradition was not enough. All too easily it could
become blurred and distorted, even falsified, with the passing of the
years.

During the last century and more, the criticism of the Gospels
has been searching in its intensity. It is a far cry from the days when
we could think of them as four independent portraits of Jesus. It is

[2] Jerome, *Commentary on Galations* 6:10

abundantly clear that they are not portraits at all—in the modern sense of that term. Nor are they independent of one another, though the nature of their interdependence is still a matter for hot debate and is likely to continue to be for a long time to come. But even within half a lifetime the approach to the criticism of the Gospels has changed enormously. B. H. Streeter's *The Four Gospels*, first published in 1924, massive and influential as it was in its detailed comparative work, does not satisfy us today. The four-document theory (Mark, the earliest Gospel, used by Matthew and Luke; Q, the sayings source with the outline of a story; M, matter peculiar to the first Gospel, and L, matter peculiar to the third) leaves too many questions unanswered. Source criticism is not enough. Indeed there are some who say that such an approach to the Gospels should be regarded as a thing of the past. So Xavier Léon-Dufour can write, '. . . the theory of "Two Sources" (Mark and "Q") must be regarded as a hypothesis which served a very useful purpose in its day, but which ought to be consigned to an honourable grave.'[3] He goes on, 'The age when scholars argued interminably whether Matthew or Mark wrote first ought to be considered as over: it did not, in any case, contribute much of spiritual value to the ordinary Christian.'[4] Many would regard these sentences as an overstatement or at least as an over-simplification. But they point to the fact that the most recent work on the Gospels has led to the posing of a different set of questions, which in turn has led to an approach to the Gospels which has produced some results which may well prove to be of abiding value.

Léon-Dufour, in the book to which reference has just been made, argues with force that the story of the Gospels, with their tantalising parallels and differences, only comes to life when it is seen against the background of the living Church, a Church at worship, a Church getting on with the job of catechising and of preaching to all nations. This is surely true. The strata that go to the make-up of the Gospels came into being as a result of the kind of questions which we have posed in this chapter—the question of

[3] Léon-Dufour, *The Gospels and the Jesus of History* (Collins, 1968), p. 191

[4] ibid., p. 192

continuity in spite of the non-appearance of Jesus on the clouds of heaven and in spite of man's transitoriness, the question of how things began, the question of what to preach and what to teach.

The argument of Léon-Dufour, of course, is not new. J. Rendel Harris as long ago as 1916, in his book *Testimonies*, put forward the view that Christians of the New Testament period used 'testimony books'—anthologies of Old Testament passages which were regarded as significant for Christians. A. Lukyn Williams, writing in 1935, thought that we can 'hardly be wrong in considering that the writers of the New Testament had at their disposal collections of what we call proof texts from the Old Testament'.[5] He does not envisage one *Book of Testimonies*, but 'catena after catena of texts from the Old Testament which were regarded as *Testimonies* to Christ and Christianity', the Old Testament being 'treated as little more than an arsenal of separate weapons for Christian warfare'.[6] C. H. Dodd, in a weighty chapter entitled 'Testimonies' in his *According to the Scriptures*,[7] believes that the New Testament writers worked upon 'a tradition in which certain passages of the Old Testament were treated as "testimonies" to the Gospel facts, or in other words as disclosing that "determinate counsel of God" which was fulfilled in these facts'.[8] He believes that the evidence points not so much to an anthology of single, isolated proof-texts, as to 'the hypothesis that there were some parts of scripture which were early recognised as appropriate sources from which *testimonia* might be drawn'.[9]

It would seem to be abundantly clear that behind our Gospels we must see a desire to meet preaching and catechetical needs and to do so in the light cast by recent Messianic events on the Jewish Scriptures.

Thus the Gospel according to St. Mark is best seen as material for the catechist and the evangelist, the material that goes to the make-up of the Gospel being grouped round certain points of

[5] A. Lukyn Williams, *Adversus Judaeos* (Cambridge University Press, 1935), p. 10

[6] ibid., pp. 12–13

[7] C. H. Dodd, *According to the Scriptures* (Nisbet, 1952), p. 28 ff.

[8] ibid., p. 57

[9] ibid., pp. 59–60

catechetical interest. St. Matthew is to be viewed as an aid to the preacher, the teaching of and the narratives about our Lord being set in a catechetical framework, a kind of lectionary to be read and interpreted. St. Luke, though he has a very different kind of reader in mind from that of St. Matthew, is expounding a theological theme, interpreting for Christians far from the 'beginning of things' what the meaning of these events and their teaching is in the light of Easter Day. And what is true of the Synoptic Gospels is even more abundantly true of the Fourth, that 'interpretative expression of a memory' as William Temple called it,[10] which quite openly was written with an evangelistic and apologetic purpose in mind—'in order that you may hold the faith that Jesus is the Christ, the Son of God, and that through this faith you may possess life by his name'.[11]

Even in the Epistles it is possible to detect a liturgical and catechetical purpose. Not only are there fragments of hymns which probably reflect the worship of the early Church, such as

> Awake, sleeper,
> rise from the dead,
> and Christ will shine upon you,[12]

and early creedal formulae such as

> He who was manifested in the body,
> vindicated in the spirit,
> seen by angels;
> who was proclaimed among the nations,
> believed in throughout the world,
> glorified in high heaven.[13]

There are 'catechetical patterns or Forms underlying the Epistles', as the late Dean of Winchester made abundantly clear in a full and

---

[10] William Temple, *Readings in St. John's Gospel* (Macmillan, 1939), p. 105
[11] John 20:31 N.E.B.
[12] Eph. 5:14 N.E.B.
[13] 1 Tim. 3:16 N.E.B.

learned essay in his Commentary on the First Epistle of St. Peter.[14] His indebtedness to the earlier work of Dr. Philip Carrington's *The Primitive Christian Catechism* and to A. M. Hunter's *Paul and his Predecessors* is acknowledged by him in his commentary *passim*. Dr. Selwyn writes, 'Modern missionary methods make it likely that these [catechetical forms] were numerous, being freely divided or put together to meet local needs. The question as to whether they were oral or written is somewhat unreal, since the probability is that enough copies became available in manuscript for the Church's missionaries (and some at least of the local presbyters) to possess one each, while the rank and file of converts were content with an oral knowledge of the tradition.'[15]

That is well said, and points to the emergence, very early in the life of the Christian Church, of collections of sayings, of parables, of forms, of stories (and especially of the Passion story) which, beginning in an oral form, soon took written shape. Such began to emerge probably long before the Epistles came to be written; and it must, of course, be remembered that the Pauline letters preceded the earliest of the Gospels, St. Mark.

The Epistles themselves were designed to be read in churches. Sometimes the writer, St. Paul for example, had one church or one group of churches only in mind—the Epistle to the Galatians, with its excoriating denunciations and its notes of tenderness, was meant for Galatian readers and hearers only. But some of the New Testament letters were written with a wider audience in view. Ephesians was almost certainly an encyclical letter—the earliest manuscripts omit the words 'in Ephesus',[16] and the personal references which are the mark of many letters are almost wholly lacking. Colossians, too, was meant for more than Colossian needs—'see that it is also read to the congregation at Laodicea', the writer instructs the Colossians,[17] and it may be doubted whether its journey stopped even in Laodicea; it is more than likely that copies were made and circulated fairly widely in what we now call Asia Minor.

[14] E. G. Selwyn, *The First Epistle of St. Peter* (Macmillan, 1946), pp. 363–466.
[15] ibid., p. 18
[16] Eph. 1:1
[17] Col. 4:16 N.E.B.

To recapitulate: a picture is beginning to emerge with a considerable degree of clarity. It is the picture of an infant Church going to its two-fold task of worship and evangelism with a liveliness inspired by the Holy Spirit and a gusto which was like a breath of new life in a weary world. Armed with word and sacrament and with the marks of a holy life, the Church realised that this, mighty though it was, was not enough if its members, and especially its new recruits, were to continue to fulfil the task laid upon them by their Lord. They must have in their hand something written, by its nature unchangeable and permanent, something which would be adequate, when the living and abiding voice of the first apostles was stilled for ever, to give to succeeding generations the essence of what they had received from their Lord.

Part of this need was met by the Septuagint, that translation of the Old Testament Scriptures which could be almost universally understood because it was in Greek, the lingua franca of the world of the first century. That was a great deal, but it was not enough. Hence the need for, and the emergence of, lists of proof-texts, an early story (or early stories) of the Passion, collections of sayings and parables of Jesus often in a shape easily memorised, catechetical and creedal and hymnal forms. Then came the Epistles, of which our New Testament ones are doubtless only a fraction. Then came the Gospels, the four retained in our New Testament again being not the only ones written but standing out head and shoulders above the others and enduring by a kind of combination of the grace of God and the survival of the fittest.

It was not long before the New Testament canon was completed —or almost so, for there were a few books (such as 2 Peter and the Revelation) about whose inclusion there continued to be doubt for some time. But about the main body of the New Testament—the Gospels and the Acts and the Epistles—there was little if any doubt pretty early in the second century.

Thus the Church was equipped with the Scriptures, the books of the Old and New Testaments which, in the succeeding centuries, were to be at once her main weapon in her warfare against the forces of evil, and the measure by which her doctrine and the life of her members was to be judged. Thus the members of the Church became the people of a book, and that book the Bible. Without its written guidance, they might—indeed they almost certainly would —have gone far astray from the central facts and teachings of a faith grounded in history.

3

'Every Man in his Own Language'

'All except the apostles were scattered over the country districts of Judaea and Samaria . . . As for those who had been scattered, they went through the country preaching the Word.'[1] Persecution was the best thing that could have happened to the early Church. It would have been easy for its members to settle down comfortably in Jerusalem, to continue with the Temple services, and to nourish themselves on word and sacrament, while they awaited the coming of the Lord. Violent persecution put an end to any such disastrous possibility. The wrath of man was turned to the praise of God. Had not the command been given to 'go forth and make all nations' disciples of Christ? Persecution gave just the needed thrust to obedience, and the Church became what it was always meant to be, a missionary and an evangelising Church.

It went to its task, as we have seen, well equipped. The Spirit had been given and so the Church had divine inspiration. It found its strength in the sacraments, and as it ministered the word it discovered that that ministry, like mercy, 'blesseth him that gives, and him that takes'. As years went by, its literary equipment—if that phrase be not taken to indicate too much—increased; one centre might have more than another by way of apostolic letters or collections of texts, sayings, parables, and so forth. But before many decades were past, it is likely that most churches had something very like what we now know as the Bible, and had it in the lingua franca of the day, Greek. We cannot be dogmatic on this point. It is altogether probable that the situation varied considerably between the churches. The members of one church might be predominantly illiterate, and would be dependent on the reading and exposition of a few members or even of one member better equipped than the others. Another church might have a greater

[1] Acts 8:1, 4 N.E.B.

proportion of well educated members. Often it would happen that a group of churches in a locality—say, in Asia Minor—would share what literary treasures they possessed. For we must not forget that, in days long before the invention of printing, the copying out by hand of manuscripts was an arduous and tedious task. But the copying began and went on, giving rise, as all textual scholars know, to differences small and great in the copies made and circulated.

The position is not clear in its details, but the overall picture is clear enough—there was a period of what we might call literary fluidity, the 'equipment' varying from place to place, until the time arrived when, scarce though the copies might be, the Bible as we now know it came to be regarded as the authentic Scriptures of the Christian Church, its guide and nourishment, to be read and expounded in its liturgical worship, and to be the indispensable instrument of its evangelistic thrust and outreach.

We have seen that part of the preparation for the coming of Christ was the translation of the Old Testament into Greek and that this was probably completed at any rate by the year 132 B.C. We have seen that all the books of the New Testament were also written in Greek. But we also know that, in the early centuries of the expansion of the Christian Church, these Greek Scriptures were translated into other languages. Thus we have, for example, the Syriac Bible and the Latin Bible, not to mention the Coptic and Ethiopic Versions. Why was it that there was a need for these great Versions, as they were called, when Greek was the lingua franca of the world?

The answer would seem to be roughly along these lines. It is true that, around the first century of our era, 'the Babel of tongues was hushed in the beautiful language of Greece'. But that does not indicate by any means that all other languages died out. Far from it. For example, our Lord spoke Aramaic, though it is pretty certain that he understood a good deal of Greek—this would have been helpful, if not entirely necessary, when he crossed the Jordan into the Decapolis area ('Decapolis' being Greek for 'ten cities'). To speak of him as bi-lingual might be an exaggeration; to conceive of him as having a slight acquaintance with Greek is wholly likely.

Now this was a situation which obtained further afield from the place of origin of Christianity. For example, in and around Urfa (the ancient Edessa, the capital of Osrhoene in northern Mesopotamia), Syriac continued to be spoken. No doubt Greek was also known in the area, but if the people were to have the Bible in the language with which they were most familiar, in 'their own tongue', then a translation would be called for. Again, we have seen that St. Paul wrote to the Romans in Greek; Ignatius did likewise some fifty years later. That was because a knowledge of Greek formed an essential part of the education of the upper classes at Rome and because the slaves and freedmen were mostly Greek in origin, Latin being to them largely an unknown tongue. But slowly and surely Latin made its way and Greek declined. In North Africa Latin seems to have been from very early times the only language. Hence the need for a translation—a 'version'—of the Greek Scriptures into the language of the people. It was unthinkable that there should be a Church which did not have the Scriptures in the language of the people to whom it ministered. Such versions were regarded as indispensable if the evangelistic and pastoral and liturgical work of the Church was to go forward.

The fact that these versions were regarded as indispensable to the life and work of the Church is attested by the early dates when they were made. We cannot be exact in the dates we assign to these translations but it is commonly accepted that the Peshitta (Syriac) Version, which even to this day is the official Bible of the Indian Church, was current during the second or early third century. It is likely that the Gospels were translated from Greek into Syriac as early as the first half of the second century and the Acts and the Epistles at any rate not much later.

The first Latin translation, the Vulgate, which is associated with the name of Jerome (born *c.* A.D. 346) did not appear till the latter part of the fourth century—the whole undertaking being completed in A.D. 405. But that does not mean that the churches whose members spoke Latin went without a translation of the Scriptures into their own tongue until Jerome produced his famous work. On the contrary; it was precisely because there were so many Latin translations, each differing from the other, that Pope Damasus asked Jerome, Western Christendom's greatest scholar of the period, to produce an authoritative version of the Latin New Testament. Augustine has a comment worthy of note; he wrote, 'In the early days of the faith, no sooner did anyone gain possession of a Greek manuscript, and imagine himself to have any facility in both languages (however slight that might be), than he made bold to translate it.'[2] The picture painted by Augustine is highly interesting. We can see the way in which Latin-speaking Christians were seized of the necessity of their little Christian communities having the Scriptures in the language they best understood and most commonly used. The translations may have led to a measure of textual chaos and to a crop of inaccuracies, but their existence makes it abundantly clear that such translations were regarded as essential to the life and welfare of the communities for whom they were made. The Church must go to its work with a Bible in its hand, and that Bible must be in the language of the people.

What has been written of the Syriac and Latin versions is also true of the Coptic versions, designed for Christians whose native tongue was Egyptian. All these versions were, in the words of Professor B. M. Metzger, 'products of the missionary activities of Christian evangelists and their converts in various lands to which the Gospel had been carried'.[3]

To turn from the world of the ancient versions to that of the English versions is to experience an immense change of atmosphere but, at the same time, to see exactly the same principle at work—the conviction, operating in men of a wide variety of backgrounds and of spiritual experience, that the Bible must be given to the people, freely, and in their own tongue.

The story of the presentation of the message of the Bible to the English people is a very long one. Nor is that to be wondered at. It is surely misleading to speak, as Sir William A. Craigie does in his essay on 'The English Versions (to Wyclif)', of the introduction of Christianity into England by St. Augustine in 596, as if this were

[2] Augustine, *de doctr. Christ.*, ii, 11
[3] Writing in Peake's *Commentary on the Bible* (Nelson, revised edn. 1962), p. 671

some new thing.[4] Christianity had been introduced to England centuries before that. Were there not three English bishops (Eborius of York, Restitutus of London, and Adelphius possibly of Caerleon) at the Council of Arles in A.D. 314? Is it not likely that Christianity in these islands came in the wake of the Roman legions, or, indeed, may have been introduced by Roman soldiers who came to Britain as disciples of Jesus Christ? Whatever may have been the way, or ways, in which the Christian faith first crossed from the Continent to Britain, it is certain that its evangelists would be seeking the best possible means by which to make vividly real 'the greatest drama ever staged'. Those whom they sought to reach would, no doubt, for the most part have been illiterate. Is it not more than probable that some kind of dramatic presentation of the Faith took place very early?

It is, of course, a fact that Baptism and the Eucharist were themselves dramatic re-presentations of the central facts of our redemption, 'shewings forth' of the mighty acts of God in Christ. Dr. F. W. Dillistone, in his *The Christian Understanding of Atonement*, has an important section on this matter. 'The Christian Church,' he writes, 'went forward from the apostolic age possessing two treasures of supreme value—its own distinctive documents at the heart of which was the Passion Story, and the Hebrew Scriptures at the heart of which was the record of a covenant sealed and renewed by sacrifice. *Each of these had powerful dramatic qualities :* each was related to what may be called a symbolic or sacramental pattern of social behaviour. *It is no cause for surprise therefore that in a comparatively short time the sacramental life of the Christian society became regularised and to some extent formalised.*'[5] Dr. Dillistone goes on to speak of the Church providing 'opportunities for dramatic participation in sacramental ceremonies bearing a transcendent significance ... In baptism there was the obvious symbolism of the cleansing effected by water, especially running water, but in addition there were ceremonies of exorcism involving the use of breath and fire and the symbolic use of light to drive

---

[4] In *Ancient and English Versions of the Bible*, ed. H. Wheeler Robinson (Oxford University Press, 1940), p. 128

[5] p. 141 (my italics)

away darkness.'[6] He then traces the gradual growth of the liturgy and especially of the Eucharistic liturgy '. . . in the East the liturgy was . . . a re-enactment of the total passion story and this fulfilled, at least to a degree, the Day of Atonement ceremonies with which the Church was familiar through its possession of the Old Testament scriptures.'[7] He makes the point that the form of service which had been established by the time of St. Chrysostom has to a remarkable extent remained unchanged down to the present day. Moreover the very structure and furnishing of the church are highly symbolic, and the ultimate mystery of the Divine Presence is felt intensely but never expressed in words.

Such sacramental dramatic 're-enactments' as we have just been touching on were patient of almost endless development. Indeed, from the earliest days art came to the assistance of Christian evangelism in predominantly non-literary ages. The mosaics which archaeologists have uncovered in Israel and which delight the eye of the tourist today illustrate the point. (One thinks, for example, of the Byzantine mosaic floor in the Church of the Multiplication of the Loaves and Fishes at Tabgha.) What G. M. Trevelyan wrote of England in the fourteenth century was substantially true of many other parts of Europe long before that period: 'The peasant as he stood or knelt on the floor of the church each Sunday, could not follow the Latin words, but good thoughts found a way into his heart as he watched what he revered and heard the familiar yet still mysterious sounds. Around him blazed on the wall frescoes of scenes from the scriptures and the lives of saints; and over the rood loft was the Last Judgment depicted in lively colours, paradise opening to receive the just, and on the other side flaming hell with devil executioners tormenting naked souls.'[8]

Mr. Robert Speaight[9] sees in the *Quem Quaerites* the first Christian plays. This was a kind of dialogue which took place in monastic choirs in the small hours of Easter morning, when the following was recited:

[6] ibid., p. 143
[7] ibid., pp. 143–4
[8] G. M. Trevelyan, *English Social History* (Longmans, 1942), pp. 44–45
[9] Robert Speaight, *The Christian Theatre* (Burns and Oates, 1966), p. 10

'Every Man in his Own Language'

Q.   Whom do you seek in the sepulchre, O Christians?

A.   Jesus of Nazareth, who was crucified, O heavenly ones.

Q.   He is not here; he is risen even as he said before.
      Go, proclaim that he has risen from the grave.

Thus the liturgical plays developed, so loved of the English people between the eleventh and fifteenth centuries. It is all to the good that the performance of cycles of Mystery Plays has in recent years been revived, due in large part to the researches and enthusiasm of the late Canon J. S. Purvis. His book *From Minster to Market Place*[10] provides an admirable account of the largest of all the medieval play-cycles, that of York, over an unbroken period of roughly four centuries.

When in the twentieth century we recall how George Bell, Dean of Canterbury and later Bishop of Chichester, encouraged men like T. S. Eliot, Christopher Fry, Charles Williams and Christopher Hassall by putting on their plays in Canterbury Cathedral;[11] when we remember that, during the Second World War, Dorothy Sayers' *The Man Born to be King* reached millions over the radio; when, every decade, we see tens of thousands flocking to the Passion Play at Oberammegau, we are simply watching the continuation in modern days of that marriage of the arts with evangelism which began in earliest times.

It is not altogether easy to trace the beginnings of the actual translation of the Scriptures from the Latin into the language of the English people. Bede's work, of which we shall shortly have more to say, was certainly preceded by an era of biblical paraphrases into the vernacular. Perhaps the most famous of these were the paraphrases of Caedmon (*fl.* 680), a brother from the abbey of the Lady Hilda at Whitby. Of him the charming story is told that he felt keenly his inability to sing, and so would leave the table when he saw the harp coming his way.

But one night when he had done so, and had lain down in the stable and there fallen asleep, there stood One by him in a

[10] Published posthumously by St. Anthony's Press, York, 1969
[11] See Ronald C. D. Jasper, *George Bell* (Oxford University Press, 1967), chapter 7

dream, and said, 'Caedmon, sing Me something.' And he answered, 'I cannot sing, and for that reason I have left the feast.' But He said, 'Nevertheless, thou canst sing to Me.' 'What,' said he, 'must I sing?' And He said, 'Sing the beginning of created things.' So he sang; and the poem of Caedmon is the first native growth of English literature. It is a paraphrase in verse of the Bible narrative, from both Old and New Testaments, written in that early dialect which we call Anglo-Saxon, but which is really the ancient form of English.[12]

We may well believe, indeed, that, long before the period of Caedmon and Bede, the Scriptures had been partially paraphrased and translated into the native tongue. We know, for example, that while Bede was still a young man, there was a translation of the Psalms made by Aldhelm, Bishop of Sherborne (d. 709). The many early versions which have come down to us show that the primitive Church knew nothing of the later tradition, which prevailed over Western Christendom for a thousand years and more, that Latin, and Latin only, was the sacred language of religion. 'The seed in secret grew' in the early centuries; the 'blade' appeared with the tentative efforts of Caedmon, Bede, King Alfred (who, according to William of Malmesbury, attempted to translate the Psalter but died when he had 'barely finished the first part'), and others; but it was only with the coming of Wycliffe that 'the full corn in the ear' was produced.

Bede (673–735), well called 'the Venerable', has been described by Sir Frederick G. Kenyon as 'the glory of the Northumbrian School, which . . . was the most shining light of learning in Western Europe during the eighth century'.[13] Though, apparently, his translations from the Scriptures into the vernacular were fragmentary, and though no trace of them remains, we know that he was anxious that the people should have the Scriptures, at least in part, in their own tongue, in contrast to the Latin which had so far held the field. His life was one of devotion to sacred learning. Referring

[12] Sir F. G. Kenyon, *Our Bible and the Ancient Manuscripts* (Eyre and Spottiswoode, 4th revised edn., 1939), p. 195
[13] ibid.

to his life spent in the monastery of St. Paul at Jarrow on the Tyne, he wrote, 'I spent all my years in that monastery, ever intent upon the study of the Scriptures. In the intervals between the duties enjoined by the disciplinary rule and the daily care of chanting in the church, I took sweet pleasure in always learning, teaching, or writing.' It is a pleasant picture, as is the one which Cuthbert, his faithful disciple, has given us of the scholar's closing hours. It was Ascension Day, 735 (according to the Church's reckoning; the Eve of Ascension Day, according to the civil reckoning). Bede was in his cell, translating St. John's Gospel into English.

In the evening, his boy-scribe said to him, 'One sentence, dear master, is left unfinished.' He bade him write quickly. Soon the boy announced that it was finished. 'True,' the dying man said, 'it is finished. Take mine head between thy hands and raise me. Full fain would I sit with my face to my holy oratory, where I was ever wont to pray, that sitting so I may call on my Father.' And so he sat on the floor of his cell, and chanted 'Glory be to the Father and to the Son and to the Holy Ghost.' And as he breathed the words 'the Holy Ghost,' he died.[14]

The period between Bede's end and that of Wycliffe, the eighth to the fourteenth century, was an unproductive one so far as translations of the Bible into the vernacular were concerned. Mention must, of course, be made of the lovely Lindisfarne Gospels, a Latin manuscript of the late seventh century which was glossed by Aldred, Bishop of Durham, in the tenth century in Anglo-Saxon, and, about the same time, of a complete translation of the four Gospels into West Saxon. We should also note the outstanding work of Abbot Ælfric just before the end of the first millennium. He translated considerable parts of the Old Testament and the four Gospels and wrote extensive biblical homilies. He had a simple and easy style, and his work, apparently the result of lay demands, had a wide circulation. His name stands out in these centuries,

[14] From a letter written by Cuthbert to his friend Cuthwin, quoted by Leo Sherley-Price in his translation of Bede's *History of the English Church and People* (Penguin Classics, p. 18 ff.).

partly because of the sheer excellence of the work he did, and partly because there were so few others engaged on a similar task. The Church of the day had no great desire for, or confidence in, the worthwhileness of translations into the vernacular—it feared that such translations, and the glosses too, might be cited in support of popular views which did not agree with the teaching of the Church. It was a risky thing to allow the laity to think for themselves under the direct impact of the Scriptures!

G. M. Trevelyan has summarised the situation in fourteenth-century England thus: 'The peasant knew some of the sayings of Christ, and incidents from his life and from those of the Saints, besides many Bible stories such as Adam and Eve, Noah's flood, Solomon's wives and wisdom, Jezebel's fate, Jephthah and his daughter "the which he loved passing well". All these and much more with many strange embellishments, he learnt from "pious chansons" and from the friars' sensational and entertaining sermons. He never saw the Bible in English, and if he had he could not have read it. There was nothing in his own home analogous to family prayers and Bible reading. But religion and the language of religion surrounded his life. The crucifixion was often before his eyes, and the story of the crucifixion in his mind.'[15]

[15] op. cit., p. 45

4

'Deathless Minds which Leave . . . a Path of Light'

John Wycliffe

To come out of this long and dreary period into the age of Wycliffe is like emerging from a dark forest into the sunshine of open country.

It is not necessary here to tell again the story of the life of Wycliffe, 'the last of the Schoolmen and the first of the Reformers', Fellow and, for a short time Master, of Balliol College, Oxford and Rector of Lutterworth in the county of Leicestershire. The standard works of G. Lechler[1] and of H. B. Workman[2] give us all the detail we need.[3] But something must be said about the translation of the Bible which bears his name.

It is more accurate to speak of 'the Bible which bears his name' than to say 'the translation of the Bible which he himself made'. For while there is no question that the project was inspired by him and had his assistance and support, yet it is doubtful how much of this version was actually translated by Wycliffe himself. It may be that Wycliffe himself provided a version of the New Testament, but evidence is not sufficient to enable us to be dogmatic.[4] The major part of the Old Testament was translated by Nicholas

[1] G. Lechler, *John Wiclif and his English Precursors* (Religious Tract Society, revised edn., 1884)
[2] H. B. Workman, *John Wyclif* (Oxford University Press, 2 vols., 1926)
[3] For a brief summary of his life and thought, the reader should consult G. M. Trevelyan, *England in the Age of Wycliffe* (Longmans, Green 1909, new edn.) pp. 169–82.
[4] C. C. Butterworth, *The Literary Lineage of the King James Bible* (University of Pennsylvania Press), p. 41; cf. Forshall and Madden, *The Holy Bible made from the Latin Vulgate by John Wycliffe and his Followers* (Oxford University Press, 1850), vol. 1, p. vi.

Hereford, who had been a supporter of Wycliffe at Oxford.[5] The New Testament first appeared about 1380; the whole work was finished about 1382, some two years before the death of Wycliffe. It should be added that, within four years of his death, a revision of this translation appeared. This was made by a pupil of Wycliffe, most probably John Purvey, and very soon came to supersede its predecessor.

This Bible, appearing as it did at the end of Wycliffe's life, was a fitting climax to a brilliant career. Wycliffe's conviction, which had grown with the passing of the years, that the authority of the Church could no longer be accepted as final in matters of doctrine, led naturally to his more weighty reliance on the authority of Scripture. Further, his conviction of the ignorance of the clergy (which indeed needed no great powers of observation to deepen), drove him more and more to see the need for the dissemination of the Bible in the language of the people. A Wycliffe tract says, 'Many curates cannot construe nor expound their Paternoster, nor Ave, nor Creed, nor the Ten Commandments, nor many other things that they are bound to know and teach others as the Law showeth.' Instances of a similar nature could be multiplied almost indefinitely.

It is interesting that, of the copies of the Wycliffe Bible which are now extant, many are small, unadorned and closely written. This serves to show that they were intended, not for the great people and institutions (though there were copies for such), but for 'the man in the street' who could read. And for those who could *not* read— and they were the vast majority—there were the 'poor priests' from whose lips the people might learn that which Scholasticism had withheld from them, the great spiritual principles of the Bible. It was a matter of immense moment that 'the leading English thinker of his age' should deem 'no pains too great to make himself intimately familiar with the moral teaching of a book which the large majority of his fellow theologians were disposed to value chiefly as a treasure-house of dead dogma',[6] and to pass on his knowledge to all who had ears to hear. The issuing of such a translation of the

[5] *vide infra*, p. 44–45
[6] H. W. Hoare, *Our English Bible* (John Murray, 1911), p. 75

Bible—made, as we should say today, unscientifically from a Latin version which was itself in many respects corrupt—was, nevertheless, a mighty protest against superstition, and a powerful instrument in the evangelisation of the people. Made about a hundred years before the introduction of printing into England by Caxton, it yet reached multitudes by the two avenues of reading and preaching. Nothing could stop it, not even the decree, passed by the University of Oxford twenty years after Wycliffe's death, that no man should learn Holy Writ for nine or ten years after entering the University.[7] Wycliffe—and his work was an example of this—was one of those who, in Wordsworth's great phrase, 'breathe the sweet air of futurity'.[8] He was a man before his time, one of the Church's pioneers. He 'anticipated all the main positions of the Protestant Reformation'. He drew 'in anticipation the whole map of Protestant thought and belief'.[9]

In these days when copies of the Bible abound in all manner of translations, when we can buy them cheaply and read them freely, we tend to forget at what cost these privileges have been obtained for us. This being so, it is well to recall the story of the three men whose names have been mentioned as being most closely associated with the Wycliffe Bible, John Wycliffe himself, Nicholas Hereford and John Purvey. Taking them in the inverse order:

John Purvey, who at Oxford had been Wycliffe's follower and secretary, lodged with him in his last home, the Lutterworth Rectory, and constantly attended his master till the end, helping him with his literary labours. But, while Wycliffe was allowed to spend his last days in peace, though in comparative obscurity, Purvey, soon after the death of his master, entered on a period of trouble and persecution. After leaving Lutterworth, he continued his work as one of the 'poor preachers', but the Bishop of Worcester soon cut this activity short, and his books were put on the list of those which were ordered to be seized. In 1390 he was imprisoned, but continued his writing activities. Eleven years later, threatened

[7] Robert Vaughan, *The Life and Opinions of John de Wycliffe, D.D.* (1831), vol. II, p. 50

[8] William Wordsworth, *The Excursion*, IX:25

[9] H. A. L. Fisher, *A History of Europe* (Edwards Arnold, 1936), pp. 335, 350

before Convocation with death by burning, he recanted, thus saving himself from the fate which but three days previously had befallen William Sawtrey. The latter had been burned for teaching that 'after the consecration by the priest there remaineth true material bread'. The Primate, Arundel, had brought about his burning, in virtue of a writ from the King after condemnation by Convocation, while the first statute imposing death for heresy (*De Haeretico Comburendo*) was before Parliament. By recantation Purvey saved his body from the flames, but not his mind from the tortures of conscience. His resignation, after little more than two years, from the vicariate of the church to which he had been inducted after his recantation, would seem to indicate a conscience ill at ease. It may be pointed out that the recantation of Purvey casts an aspersion not primarily on him but on the persecuting church which forced him to recant. The use of terror and cruelty to break the human spirit demonstrates the need of the Church for the Bible which enshrines the principle of freedom of belief and judgement. There is evidence to show that, although released after recantation, Purvey finally died 'either in some bishop's gaol or in hiding, with none to tell his fate'.[10]

Something of his spirit can be felt in his description of what the man should be like who undertakes to translate the Bible.

'A translatour hath nede to lyve a clene lif, and be ful devout in preiers, and have not his wit ocupied about worldi thingis, that the Holi Spiryt, autour of wisdom and kunnyng and truthe, dresse him in his werk and suffre him not for to erre. By this manner, and with good lyving and greet travel, men moun come to trewe and cleer translating, and a trewe undurstonding of Holi Writ, seme it nevere so hard at the bigynnyng. God graunte to us alle grace to kunne wel and kepe wel Holi Writ, and suffre ioiefulli sum peyne for it at the laste. Amen.'

The career of *Nicholas Hereford*, the second of the three men most closely associated with the Wycliffe Bible, was no less stormy than that of John Purvey. His close association with Wycliffe at

[10] H. B. Workman, op. cit., vol. II, p. 170

Oxford and his suspension, with him and others, from all public
functions in 1382, was but the beginning of a life of persecution
both in Rome, where he made an appeal to the Pope, and in
England, where he was imprisoned and where, with John Purvey,
he recanted at Paul's Cross.

John Wycliffe himself, as was said above, closed his life in peace.
Fuller comments quaintly, 'Admirable that a hare so often hunted
with so many packs of dogs should die at last quietly sitting in his
form' (lair). That was in 1384. A posthumous condemnation of
Wycliffe by the Council of Constance in 1415 led to the order
being given that his writings were to be burnt and 'his bones to be
dug up and cast out of the consecrated ground . . .' No action,
however, was taken for some years. But in 1427 Pope Martin V
ordered Fleming, Bishop of Lincoln, 'to proceed in person to the
place where John Wycliffe is buried, cause his body and bones to
be exhumed, cast far from ecclesiastical burial and publicly burnt,
and his ashes to be so disposed of that no trace of him shall be seen
again'. This was done early in 1428.

There is something childishly pathetic about this act, supervised
as it was by men of eminent position. 'The offence which tally-
ho'ed them down to Lutterworth in a pack (Sumner, Commissary,
Chancellor, Proctors, Doctors) there to dig up his bones, burn
them and cast the ashes into Swift brook, lay in his having, with
helpers, unlocked the Bible to the common English reader.' Such
was the verdict of a modern scholar, Sir Arthur Quiller-Couch.[11]
'Thus,' wrote Thomas Fuller in 1655,[12] referring to the river Swift,
'this brook hath conveyed his ashes into Avon; Avon into Severn;
Severn into the narrow seas; they into the main ocean. And thus
the ashes of Wycliff are the emblem of his doctrine, which now is
dispersed all the world over.' A different view was held by others.
'His vile corpse they consigned to hell, and the river absorbed his
ashes.' So wrote Thomas Netter[13] of his death. 'This Master John

[11] Lately Edward VII Professor of English Literature, Cambridge
University
[12] Thomas Fuller, *The Church-History of Britain*, Bk. IV, sec. ii, par. 53,
p. 171
[13] Thomas Netter, *Doctrinalis fidei Ecclesiae Catholicae contra Wit-
clevistas et Hussitas*, vol. III, p. 830

Wycliffe translated into the Anglic, not Angelic tongue, the Gospel. Whence it is made vulgar by him, and more open to the reading of lay men and women, than it usually is to the knowledge of lettered and intelligent clergy, and thus the pearl is cast abroad and trodden under feet of swine. The jewel of the Church is turned into the common sport of the people.' So wrote Knighton[14] of his life work.

We may think of Wycliffe toiling in his last days in his rectory at Lutterworth, inspired by the principle which he expressed in the words, 'Christ and His apostolis taughten ye puple in yat tunge yat was moost knowan to yc puple. Why shulden not men nou do so?' Tennyson put it well:

—Not least art thou, thou little Bethlehem
In Judah, for in thee the Lord was born;
Nor thou in Britain, little Lutterworth,
Least, for in thee the word was born again.

Heaven-sweet Evangel, ever-living word,
Who whilome spakest to the South in Greek
About the soft Mediterranean shores,
And then in Latin to the Latin crowd,
As good need was—thou hast come to talk our isle.

Hereafter thou, fulfilling Pentecost,
Must learn to use the tongues of all the world,
Yet art thou thine own witness that thou bringest
Not peace, a sword, a fire.[15]

A word should be added here with reference to the great four-volume edition of 'The Holy Bible containing the Old and New Testaments, with the Apocryphal Books, in the earliest English versions, made from the Latin Vulgate by John Wycliffe and his followers', edited by the Reverend Josiah Forshall and Sir Frederic Madden, and published by the Oxford University Press in 1850.

[14] *Chronicon*, ed. J. R. Lumby (Rolls Series, vol. 92.2, 1895), vol. II, p. 152
[15] *Sir John Oldcastle, Lord Cobham*

The work is printed in two parallel columns, the first containing
the translation which, as we saw above, was finished two years
before the death of Wycliffe, the second containing the revision
which appeared within four years of his death and which seems to
have been the work largely of John Purvey, though no doubt he was
assisted by others who probably included Nicholas Hereford. The
revision, as a comparison of it with the original translation makes
clear, aimed at and succeeded in rendering 'the version more correct, intelligible and popular; and it manifestly becomes more easy
and familiar as the translator advances'.[16] Such a revision was
particularly necessary in that part of the Old Testament—and it
was the major part—for which Nicholas Hereford had been
responsible. It 'differed in style from the rest; it was extremely
literal, occasionally obscure, and sometimes incorrect; and there
were other blemishes throughout incident to a first essay of this
magnitude, undertaken under very unfavourable circumstances, by
different persons and at different times, upon no agreed or well
defined principle'.[17] While Wycliffe did not live to see its completion, it seems probable that the suggestion of a revision may have
come from him.

William Tyndale
We turn from the latter part of the fourteenth century to the first
part of the sixteenth, and from John Wycliffe to William Tyndale.
It can be stated without fear of contradiction that there is no one
whose influence on the growth of the English Bible is in any way
comparable to his. The position of unshakeable pre-eminence
which Tyndale holds is due to at least three factors.

First, the influence of Tyndale on the English language in
general and on the Authorised Version in particular. 'It would be
true to say that his work was not so much a contribution as a
formative influence in the development of Anglo–Saxon speech.'[18]
The Times Literary Supplement, in a review of S. L. Greenslade's

[16] op. cit., vol. I, pp. xxviii–xxix
[17] ibid., Vol. I, p. xx
[18] *Tyndale Commemoration Volume*, ed. R. Mercer Wilson (R. T. S.
Lutterworth Press, 1939), p. 4

The Work of William Tindale (1938), called him 'the man who more than Shakespeare even or Bunyan has moulded and enriched our language'. The boldness of this claim is, of course, based on the influence which Tyndale's translation had on the Authorised Version. Professor C. H. Williams has pointed out that 'when the translators of the Authorised Version (1611) came to do their work, they found in Tyndale's version so much that could not be improved upon that something between seventy and ninety per cent of the text of that version is entirely taken from Tyndale's New Testament. It might be added that when changes were made the result was not always an improvement on Tyndale's original form.'[19] A few examples will suffice to show how Tyndale 'lifted the common language, in a true nobility of homeliness, up to the sublime level of the Bible'.[20] We have all, at one time or another, been moved by the simplicity and power of such phrases as 'Until the day dawn and the day-star arise in your hearts'; 'In Him we live and move and have our being'; 'For here we have no continuing city; but we seek one to come'. These and many of the phrases which are now so much part of our everyday vocabulary that we hardly associate them with the Bible, we owe to Tyndale; of the latter class we may mention, for example, 'the burden and heat of the day'; 'eat, drink and be merry'; 'the powers that be'; 'a prophet is not without honour, save in his own country'. It was Tyndale also who was responsible for the introduction into English of the word 'Jehovah'. It is probably a fact, though not an undebated one, that the modern 'Yahweh' is a more scholarly rendering.[21] But there can be little doubt as to which is the more euphonious and majestic.

Secondly, there is the fact that Tyndale was sturdily independent in his work. He translated in his Old Testament work from the

[19] C. H. Williams, *William Tyndale* (Nelson, 1969), p. 81. He proceeds to sketch the resulting influence on Milton, Bunyan and a long list of later English writers.

[20] Hoare, op. cit., p. 120

[21] Miss B. Smalley, in *The Study of the Bible in the Middle Ages* (Oxford University Press, 1941), p. 257, points out that the glossator of the Lambeth Psalter [thirteenth century] has the form IAHAVE, 'which comes very close to JAHWEH . . . The "monstrous form" Jehovah was already known to Christians in the later thirteenth century.'

Hebrew and in his New Testament work from the Greek. This is not to suggest that he despised the work that had been done before him. Far from it. He used the Vulgate, Luther's German Bible, Erasmus's famous Greek Testament (the second edition of 1519 and the third edition of 1522), and that new translation of the New Testament into Latin which Erasmus had made to the great scandal of those whose attachment to the Vulgate amounted almost to bibliolatry. He used all these, but 'as a master and not as a disciple'.[22] 'He shows every possible variety of agreement and disagreement with his originals and secondary sources, but there is an overwhelming preponderance of renderings in which the Greek alone remains his authority against the seductions of Luther and the Vulgate.'[23] He worked on sound principles of philology and grammar. His refusal to translate the Greek word *metanoein* by 'to do penance' and *presbyteros* by 'priest', and his substitution in their place of the words 'repent' and 'senior' or 'elder', was motivated not only by his anti-sacerdotal convictions but also by sound philology.

Thirdly, he had a passionate desire, like Wycliffe before him, to make the principles of the Bible available for all to learn. Still, in his day,[24] clerical ignorance was abysmal. Foxe tells of Tyndale's remark to a divine in Gloucestershire: 'If God spare my life, ere many years I will cause a boy that driveth the plough shall know more of the Scripture than thou dost.' The fine words of Tyndale's Preface to the Pentateuch[25] sum up the motive of his life: 'I perceived . . . how that it was impossible to establish the lay people in any truth except the Scripture were plainly laid before their eyes in their mother tongue, that they might see the process, order and meaning of the text.' The influence on him of master minds such as those of Erasmus and Colet and Luther is easily seen. He was

[22] B. F. Westcott, *History of the English Bible* (Macmillan, 3rd edn. revised by W. Aldis Wright, 1905), pp. 157–8

[23] J. Isaacs, *The Bible in its Ancient and English Versions*, ed. H. Wheeler Robinson (Oxford University Press, 1940), p. 157

[24] The date of his birth is uncertain; J. F. Mozley thinks 1494 'is as possible a date as any'.

[25] *Doctrinal Treatises and Introductions to Different Portions of the Holy Scriptures* (Parker Society edn.), p. 394

wholly at one with Erasmus who wrote in the *Exhortation* with which he prefaced his New Testament of 1516: 'I totally dissent from those who are unwilling that the sacred Scriptures, translated in the vulgar tongue, should be read by private individuals. I would wish even all women to read the Gospel, and the Epistles of St. Paul. I wish they were translated into all languages of the people. I wish that the husbandman might sing parts of them at his plough, and the weaver at his shuttle, and that the traveller might beguile with their narration the weariness of his way.'

The extent of Tyndale's indebtedness to Luther may be gauged by a reference to his marginal glosses and by a perusal of his Prologue to the 1534 edition of his New Testament.[26] That, like Erasmus, he was not afraid sometimes to dip his pen in vitriol when waging war against clerical ignorance and bigoted conservatism, is clear from the glosses which he delighted to put in the margin of his translation. Thus, Numbers 23:8, 'How shall I curse whom God curseth not?' (margin: 'The pope can tell how.'); Genesis 24:60, 'And they blessed Rebecca' (margin: 'To bless a man's neighbour is to pray for him, and to wish him good: and not to wag two fingers over him.'); Leviticus 21:5, 'They shall make them no baldness upon their heads' (margin: 'Of the heathen priests therefore took our prelates the ensample of their bald pates.'). The same spirit is seen in his *The Obedience of a Christian Man* (1528) where he wages war against those who would keep back the Bible from the people. 'They say it cannot be translated into our tongue it is so rude. It is not so rude as they are false liars . . . This threatening and forbidding the lay people to read the Scripture is not for the love of your souls . . . inasmuch as they permit and suffer you to read Robin Hood and Bevis of Hampton, Hercules, Hector and Troilus, with a thousand Histories and fables of love and wantonness and of ribaudry as filthy as heart can think, to corrupt the minds of youth.'

The persecution which the fulfilment of his project brought to

[26] *The New Testament* translated by William Tyndale 1534. A reprint of the edition of 1534 with Translator's Preface and Notes and the variants of the edition of 1525. Edited for the Royal Society of Literature by N. Hardy Walter (Cambridge University Press, 1938)

Tyndale is well known. His greatest work was done between 1524
and 1536 on the Continent, especially in Cologne, Worms and
Antwerp, for he found 'not only that there was no room in my lord
of London's palace to translate the New Testament, but also that
there was no place to do it in all England'. Copies of the first
edition, begun in 1525 and completed in 1526, filtered into England
in bales of cotton and by other secret means. They were burnt at
Paul's Cross at the instigation of such men as Warham (Archbishop
of Canterbury), Tunstall (Bishop of London), Wolsey and Sir
Thomas More. The expenditure by the Archbishop of some six
hundred pounds in buying up copies must have given Tyndale a
sense of unholy glee. The chronicler, Hall, tells of a similar incident
in connection with Bishop Tunstall, whom Tyndale acidly
described as 'a still Saturn that seldom speaketh, but walketh up
and down all day musing, a ducking hypocrite, made to dissemble'.
The Bishop came home from the Continent by way of Antwerp
where he arranged with a merchant named Packington to seize a
great number of New Testaments. Hall says:

> 'The Bishop, thinking he had God by the toe, when, indeed, as
> he after thought, he had the Devil by the fist, said, 'Gentle Mr.
> Packington, do your diligence and get them, and with all my
> heart I will pay whatsoever they cost you, for the books are
> erroneous and nought, and I intend surely to burn them at
> Paul's Cross.' So Packington came to William Tyndale and said,
> 'William, I know thou art a poor man, and I have gotten thee a
> merchant.' 'Who?' said Tyndale. 'The Bishop of London.' 'He
> will burn them,' said Tyndale. 'Yea, marry,' quoth Packington.
> And so forward went the bargain; the Bishop had the books,
> Packington the thanks, and Tyndale the money.'

The money, we cannot doubt, was used for reprints! It is almost
pathetic to learn of the avidity with which the people surreptitiously
bought copies for themselves, for there was a famine in the land,
'not a famine of bread, nor a thirst for water, but of hearing the
words of the Lord'.

To satisfy this famine Tyndale gave his life. He was martyred by strangulation and burning in 1536. His last prayer was, 'Lord, open the King of England's eyes.' Only a year later that prayer was answered by the royal recognition of the Coverdale Bible, as we shall see shortly. In 1535 he wrote to some person in authority words strangely reminiscent of St. Paul's letter to Timothy (2 Timothy 4), also written from prison:

I believe, right worshipful, that you are not unaware of what may have been determined concerning me. Wherefore I beg your lordship, and that by the Lord Jesus, that if I am to remain here through the winter, you will request the commissary to have the kindness to send me, from the goods of mine which he has, a warmer cap; for I suffer greatly from cold in the head, and am afflicted by a perpetual catarrh, which is much increased in this cell; a warmer coat also, for this which I have is very thin; a piece of cloth too to patch my leggings. My overcoat is worn out; my shirts are also worn out. He has a woollen shirt, if he will be good enough to send it. I have also with him leggings of thicker cloth to put on above; he has also warmer night caps. And I ask to be allowed to have a lamp in the evening; it is indeed wearisome sitting alone in the dark. But most of all I beg and beseech your clemency to be urgent with the commissary, that he will kindly permit me to have the Hebrew bible, Hebrew grammar, and Hebrew dictionary, that I may pass the time in that study. In return may you obtain what you most desire, so only that it be for the salvation of your soul. But if any other decision has been taken concerning me, to be carried out before winter, I will be patient, abiding the will of God, to the glory of the grace of my Lord Jesus Christ; whose Spirit (I pray) may ever direct your heart. Amen.   W. Tindalus.[27]

Like St. Paul before him, Tyndale had fought a good fight, he had finished his course, he had kept the faith.

With no exaggeration, G. M. Trevelyan could write of the radical intention of 'William Tyndale, as in penury and danger he translated the Bible into words of power and beauty that unborn

[27] Quoted in J. F. Mozley, *William Tyndale* (S.P.C.K., 1937), pp. 334–5

millions were to have daily on their lips, and to interpret in a hundred different ways disruptive of the past'.[28] 'Scripture made him happy', wrote Professor S. L. Greenslade, 'and there is something swift and gay in his rhythm which conveys his happiness.'[29]

Miles Coverdale

Just over a century after the death of John Wycliffe, Miles Coverdale was born (1488–1568). Again it is not necessary to tell in any detail the story of his life—that has been well done by J. F. Mozley.[30] We merely mention that in his early days he belonged to the Augustine Friars and came under the influence of Lutheran teaching and of such men as Thomas Cromwell and Sir Thomas More. This resulted in his leaving the Order and graduating at the age of forty-three from Cambridge University as bachelor of the common law. Later, he became Bishop of Exeter, but his tenure of the see was short (1551–3), for he was deprived of that office after Edward VI died and the stormy days of the reign of Mary set in. His temperament seems to have been of a gentler and more eirenic kind than was Tyndale's.

In spite of the length of time between the production of the first Wycliffe Bible (1382) and the activities of Tyndale and Coverdale, it must not be thought that the century and a half was barren so far as the story of the Bible is concerned. A dearth of actual English versions there certainly was, in contrast to the large number that appeared in the seventy-five years between the death of Tyndale and the issuing of the Authorised Version in 1611. But a period which witnessed the powerful effects of the Renaissance and which produced such men as Erasmus, Colet and More could not have been other than formative. It was as if the ground was being broken up and the soil enriched before the planting work was done by Tyndale and Coverdale.

In tracing the story of the English Bible, we cannot deal at any length with the work of Erasmus, for the chief monument of that

[28] *English Social History*, p. 95
[29] *The Cambridge History of the Bible: The West from the Reformation to the Present Day* (Cambridge University Press, 1963), p. 144
[30] J. F. Mozley, *Coverdale and his Bibles* (Lutterworth, 1953)

life of terrific energy and untiring labour was the production of his famous Greek Testament, the *Novum Instrumentum* of 1516. But if it is true to say, as does Farrar, that 'in the person of this brilliant humanist and admirable theologian "Greece rose from the dead with the New Testament in her hand" ',[31] it is obvious that no one can understand the age and work of Tyndale and Coverdale who has not some appreciation at least of Erasmus and those other two, Colet and More, whom together Seebohm has called 'The Oxford Reformers'. To illustrate: a like passion moved Erasmus as that which had moved Wycliffe before him and was to move Tyndale during the life and after the death of Erasmus. Indeed, as we have seen, it was from him that Tyndale borrowed the phrase, as from him he inherited the enthusiasm, that 'the boy that driveth the plough' should 'know more of the Scripture' than many a theologian in his day. Further, both Tyndale and Coverdale made use of the Greek Testament of Erasmus which had marked such an epoch in the history of biblical scholarship. Wycliffe, Erasmus, Coverdale and Tyndale were all bent on waging war against that clerical ignorance which was the soporific of the people and the death of true religion. Whether or no Coverdale was a pupil of Erasmus when the latter was Professor of Greek at Cambridge between 1509 and 1516, we have no means of telling. But that he shared with him many of his ideals there can be no doubt. A common passion, a common heritage, a common enemy—these three bound the men of a later generation together in a goodly fellowship with the Wycliffe who had gone before them.

The story of the Revival of Learning, and especially of the classics, which marked the close of the fifteenth century and the beginning of the sixteenth is well-known. Colet, for example, caught the contagion of the humanism which such men as Grocyn and Linacre had imbibed in Italy. The revival of interest in the classics had combined with the warmth of his Christian faith to send him back to the study of the Greek of the New Testament and to set him on fire to preach its truths to rich and poor, learned and ignorant. The effects were powerfully felt both in Oxford and at St. Paul's Cathedral, London.

[31] Farrar, *History of Interpretation* (Macmillan, 1886), p. 316

Much has been written on the subject of the revival of the classics, and its influence on the Reformation was profound. But not so much attention has been paid to the fact that this was also the time when there was taking place a revival of *Hebrew* learning. The effect of that fact upon the story of the Bible is great. After the time of Jerome, the father of the Latin Vulgate, Hebrew learning virtually ceased among Christians for one thousand years. The ignorance of it even in the fifteenth and sixteenth centuries was extraordinary. The theologians of those days regarded with suspicion any who studied it, and called it an accursed tongue. When Reuchlin (1455–1522) lectured on it at Heidelberg he had to do so secretly, and when in 1506, he published a Hebrew grammar complete with dictionary, he had to preface it with a full and emphatic notice that Hebrew is read from right to left! But he effected for the Old Testament what Erasmus did for the New—he drove people back to the original, and set a pattern for critical work on the text by luring men away from a corrupt Latin to the *Hebraica Veritas*. It is only comparatively recently that anything approaching sufficient stress has been laid on the importance of this revival of Hebrew learning in its effect on the later versions of the Bible.[32]

The royal recognition of Tyndale's Bible in 1537 was an answer to his dying prayer. Coverdale made abundant use of Tyndale's work.[33] Coverdale's was the first English Bible to circulate without hindrance from the authorities, as it was also the first *complete* printed Bible in English (the Old Testament in the Tyndale Bible was incomplete).

A Royal Licence to translate the Bible was granted to Coverdale by King Henry VIII. While Tyndale was languishing in prison at Vilvorde (he was not martyred till 1536), there were creeping into England from the Continent (probably from Zürich or Antwerp) copies of a complete English Bible bearing the date October 4th,

---

[32] See especially David Daiches, *The King James Version of the English Bible: An Account of the Development and Sources of the English Bible of 1611 with special reference to the Hebrew Tradition* (University of Chicago Press, 1941)

[33] For details see B. F. Westcott, op. cit., p. 215 ff., and C. C. Butterworth, op. cit., p. 97 ff., for careful comparisons.

1535. The printer, for obvious reasons, suppressed his own name. But it seems likely that behind the carrying out of this work of translation was the encouragement of Thomas Cromwell, who, as Secretary of State to King Henry VIII, realised at once the need of a translation and the King's detestation of that incomplete work which was associated the name of Tyndale, whom he regarded as a heretic. The sheets were bound up in England by James Nicolson, a famous publisher; and there were subsequent editions in 1536 and 1537. The 1537 edition appeared with 'the King's most gracious license', and was the forerunner of the Great Bible of 1539, the frontispiece of which (said to be designed by Hans Holbein) depicts Henry VIII handing the Bible to Cranmer, representing the clergy, and Cromwell, representing the laity.[34]

The year between the issuing of the licence and the publication of the Great Bible saw what was one of the greatest events in the whole story of the English Bible, namely, the issuing of the Royal Injunction to all clergy. This ran as follows: 'Ye shal provyde one boke of the whole Bible, in the largest volume, in Englyshe, sett up in summe convenyent place within the churche that ye have cure of, whereat your parishioners may most commodiously resort to the same and rede yt.' The effect of this Injunction was to ensure that a Bible was put in eleven thousand parish churches. The entrance of God's word thus began to give light, and that on an ample scale.

It may be a matter of disappointment to some that Coverdale's translation was by no means an independent one. Though he was not unacquainted with Hebrew, yet a comparison of his Old Testament with that of the Swiss–German version published by Zwingli and Leo Juda in 1524–9 makes his dependence on it obvious, while his New Testament is a revision of Tyndale's translation by comparison with the German. Modestly he says in his dedication of the book to the King:

But to saye the trueth before God, it was nether my laboure ner desyre, to haue this worke put in my hande: neuertheles it greued me that other nacyons shulde be more plenteously

---

[34] A reproduction of this frontispiece is given in Sir F. G. Kenyon, op. cit., plate 1, and in H. W. Hoare, op. cit., facing p. 191.

prouyded for with the scripture in theyr mother tongue, then we: therfore whan I was instantly requyred, though I coulde not do so well as I wolde, I thought it yet my dewtye to do my best, and that with a good wyll.

And again:

For the which cause (acordyng as I was desyred) I toke the more vpon me to set forth this speciall translacyon, not as a checker, not as a reprouer, or despyser of other mens translacyons (for amonge many as yet I haue founde none without occasyon of greate thankes-geuynge vnto god) but lowly and faythfully haue I folowed myne interpreters, and that vnder correccyon.

The title page bears the words 'faithfully translated out of Latin and Dutch'.

But if we, who live in an age when scientific exactitude and philological accuracy are rightly esteemed and who admire Erasmus and Tyndale for their passionate emphasis on getting back to original sources, are disappointed in the 'secondary' nature of Coverdale's translation, yet we must not think of him as merely a copyist. We value his Bible for at least four reasons. *First*, because it is to him that we owe that singularly euphonious and beautiful version of the Psalms which we have in our Prayer Book (Tyndale had not translated them), and which through constant use has become so familiar to us as a people. Coverdale 'sings his way through psalms and sentences like a chorister enjoying his anthem'.[35] He 'is almost a poet, and parts of his work have the true poetic touch. Turn to the Prayer Book version of the Psalms ... and compare them with the Psalms in any other version; you will notice the difference at once. The Prayer Book Psalms read as though they were written to be sung; their rhythmic cadences linger on the ear like the fragrance of sweet music. *Truer* the later versions may be; *poetically*—and the Hebrew Psalms are true poems—they fall short'.[36] It is significant that when, in 1958, a

[35] J. P. Hodges, *The Riches of Our Prayer Book* (S.P.C.K., 1941), p. 80
[36] A. H. Wilkinson, *Four Hundred Years of the Printed English Bible* (§6), p. 4.

small commission, whose membership included the late T. S. Eliot and the late C. S. Lewis, was appointed to revise the Psalter, its terms of reference contained the injunction '. . . to retain, as far as possible, the general character in style and rhythm of Coverdale's version and its suitability for congregational use'.

Secondly, we value Coverdale's Bible because of his felicitous use of the English language. Coverdale may not have been a great philologist. But he had that gift, which sometimes is denied to the more scientific, the ability to appreciate and sense the power of an apt phrase. He was a master of letters and possessed what Hoare in a fine sentence calls 'the mastery over what may be described as the literary semi-tone'.[37] *Thirdly*, as has been mentioned above, Coverdale's was the first *complete* English printed Bible, as Tyndale had left the Old Testament unfinished. To him, the English versions of the prophetical and poetical books of the Old Testament are primarily due. Further, it was the first complete translation from the pen of one single author. *Fourthly*, the indebtedness of the Authorised Version to Coverdale's Bible, while not being on anything approaching so large a scale as its debt to Tyndale's, yet is an appreciable one.[38] The failure of such phrases of Coverdale's as the following to get into the Authorised Version may or may not be an advantage: Psalm 91:5, 'Thou shalt not nede to be afrayed for eny bugges[39] by night'; Jeremiah 8:22, 'There is no more triacle at Galaad'. But there can be no doubt about the abiding merit of the beautiful form, so familiar to us in our Book of Common Prayer, in which Coverdale has given us the old hymn book of the Jewish Church.

From Coverdale to 1611
'There is no parallel in literary or religious history to the seventy-five years of endeavour from Tyndale's Testament of 1525 to the end of the century, nothing like this concentrated history of pioneer

[37] H. W. Hoare, op. cit., p. 178
[38] Interesting examples may be found in C. C. Butterworth, op. cit., ch. VII
[39] Bogies

endeavour and patient scholarship.' So writes Mr. J. Isaacs.[40] Certainly no chapter which seeks to carry on the story of the English Bible after the time of Tyndale and Coverdale and to describe the circumstances which gave rise to the Authorised Version can fail to take at least some notice of the unbroken line of revision which joined the year 1525 to the year 1611. But as we cast a cursory glance at the versions which constitute that unbroken line, it only makes us realise by contrast how immensely important are the dates which signalised the appearing of Tyndale's first edition and of the Authorised Version respectively.

The 'Matthew Bible', 'set forth with the King's most gracious license', appeared in 1537, the year of the Royal Injunction. This Bible consisted of all the work that Tyndale had published, together with some manuscript remains of his which had never found their way into the printer's hands, together with Coverdale's translation where Tyndale's was not available. So we have the strange phenomenon of Tyndale being martyred for his work one year, and the very next year all his work appearing with the Royal smile upon it and the blessing of Cranmer 'so far as he had read' (which probably was not far!) 'until such time that we the Bishops shall set forth a better translation, which I think will not be till a day after doomsday'. So 'God buries his workmen but carries on his work'.

It seems probable that the moving spirit behind this Bible was actually John Rogers, a faithful disciple of Tyndale who had been appointed by him as his literary executor. Certain it is that he passed all the proofs of the work, and that as he laboured on the Bible his life was changed. The association of his name with the Bible would have prejudiced its progress, because of his known friendship with Tyndale. (As a matter of fact, he was destined for a death similar to that of his master—he was burned during the Marian persecution in 1555.) So it was sent into the world under the name of Matthew, which, in the opinion of J. F. Mozley,[41] is more likely an alias for Rogers than the name of the London fishmonger and burgess of Colchester with whom it has often been associated.

[40] J. Isaacs, op. cit., p. 195
[41] J. F. Mozley, op. cit., p. 354 ff.

The main interest of the Matthew Bible centres in the fact that it is the real basis of all later revisions.

The 'Great Bible' followed the Coverdale and the Matthew Bibles in quick succession. It appeared in 1539, promoted by Thomas Cromwell and prepared by Coverdale. Based on the Matthew Bible, it had been brought into a more faithful relation to the Hebrew and Latin texts by the use of the Complutensian Polyglot and the works of many scholars, translators and editors whose books Coverdale consulted.

It got its name from the fact that it was a magnificent specimen of typography. The frontispiece, said to be designed by Hans Holbein, has already been referred to.[42] A special illuminated copy on vellum, now one of the treasures of the Library of St. John's College, Cambridge, was presented to Cromwell in 1539, as a token of appreciation for his sponsoring of the Bible.

Coming as it did so soon after the Royal Injunction, the Great Bible had a very big circulation, and passed through no less than seven editions in two years. The edition which appeared in April 1540 has these words on the title-page: 'This is the Bible apoynted to the use of the churches.'

There were other versions, such as the 'Taverner Bible' which, while fascinating for its individual touches, was so quickly superseded by the wide circulation of the Great Bible that it had not much direct effect upon later versions. But the next real landmark is 1560, the year which saw the birth of the 'Geneva Bible', popularly known (though hardly correctly, as Wycliffe had used the word himself) as the 'Breeches Bible', because of its translation in Genesis 3:7 of 'breeches' for 'aprons'. The years between the Great Bible and the Geneva Bible had been sad ones in the story of the Bible in England. After the execution of Thomas Cromwell, there was a violent reaction against the popular use, and it must be admitted sometimes abuse, of the Bible. First came the prohibition of all Tyndale Bibles; then of all Coverdale; then the restriction of the use of the Great Bible to the upper classes only. During the five years of Mary's reign (1553–8), when the authority of the Pope was restored, the English Bible was not allowed to be printed in Eng-

[42] *vide supra*, p. 56

land, and the Marian persecution led, as persecution so often does, to the reverse of what it was intended to produce, namely, a high valuation of liberty and not least liberty to read the Word of God. So it was only two years after Mary's death that the Geneva Bible was produced, a revision rather than a new translation, but a revision with which many outstanding names were connected, including those of Coverdale, Calvin, Beza and Knox. Prepared at Geneva, 'the holy city of the Alps', where there gathered in great numbers Protestants of various nationalities who had been expelled from their own countries, this revision was in the nature of a collation of the Hebrew, Greek, Latin, French and German works. Issued in convenient (quarto) size and at moderate price, divided into chapter and verse division,[43] with italics for words not in the original, and with explanatory notes, its appearance was timely and warmly welcomed. It was for fifty years the household Bible of the English people.

The 'Bishops' Bible', published in 1568, was the result of some four years' work on the part of a revision committee organised by Archbishop Parker. He was concerned at the lack of uniformity which obtained as the result of the existence side by side of the Coverdale, Matthew, Great and Geneva Bibles. The Bishops' Bible was based on the Great Bible, and, in contrast to many of its predecessors, it was agreed 'to make no bitter notes upon any text' (good precedent for the rule to be adopted many years later by the British and Foreign Bible Society, 'of which the sole object shall be to encourage the wider circulation of the Holy Scriptures, *without note or comment*'). Though it enjoyed a second edition in 1572, the version was not an outstanding one, owing largely to the fact that it was lacking in strong general editorship, with the result that it is often uneven in its quality. Perhaps its chief importance lies in the

---

[43] The Bible was divided into chapters in the thirteenth century, either by Langton, Archbishop of Canterbury, or by Cardinal Hugo de Sancto Caro, a Dominican monk. The verse divisions we owe to Robert Stephens (sixteenth century) who, as his son tells us, hastily jotted down the numbers of the verses on the margin of his Greek Testament as an occupation to beguile the tedium of a journey from Paris to Lyons, on the basis of a similar division of the Hebrew Bible made in the preceding century.

fact that the 1572 edition was used as the official basis of the Authorised Version.

The publication in 1609–10 of the Douai Old Testament (the Rheims New Testament had preceded it in 1582) brings us practically to the time of the Authorised Version. The Church of Rome felt it wise at long last, in view of the multitude of existing Protestant versions, to provide the faithful with a version of their own, made from the Vulgate and provided with abundant notes. The Preface to the King James Version gibed, 'Since they must needs translate the Bible, yet by the language thereof it may be kept from being understood.' And surely the gibe is almost deserved, for the multitude of words of Latin derivation makes it extremely difficult to read. Thus in the twenty-third Psalm, the familiar words 'my cup runneth over' (A.V.), 'my cup shall be full' (Prayer Book), are rendered 'my chalice inebriating how goodlie is it', while the 'daily bread' of the Lord's Prayer becomes 'supersubstantial bread'. Examples might be multiplied. This Roman Catholic translation, for all its literalness, was influenced not a little by the earlier English versions and especially (it would appear) by the Geneva Bible and by the Latin–English Testament which Nicolson printed for Coverdale in 1538. It is also interesting to note that, in succeeding revisions of the Rheims-Douai Version, many alterations have been made under the influence of the Authorised Version, which later took first place among all English versions. So perhaps Roman Catholic readers too must acknowledge how greatly they are in debt to Tyndale. The Rheims New Testament was used by the King James's revisers, but the Douai Old Testament appeared too late to be of use to them.

The Authorised Version

The Authorised Version of 1611 was the result of no single individual but rather of a 'multitude of counsellors' who themselves drew upon the labours of the giants whose heirs they were. Books which are the result of the collaboration of big committees often show signs of weakness—the 'seams' are all too easily visible! It is, therefore, a great tribute to John Wycliffe, Miles Coverdale and William Tyndale especially that their influence was so great that no committee could undo its work and that, on the contrary, the Authorised Version has taken such a place in our national heritage that Macaulay could describe it as 'a book which, if everything else in our language should perish, would alone suffice to show the whole extent of its beauty and power'.

The Committee (itself composed of six sub-committees, two at Westminster, two at Oxford and two at Cambridge) included some of the ablest scholars and thinkers in the country.[44] It was the King himself (James VI of Scotland and I of England) who, supporting a suggestion of a new version made at the Hampton Court Conference of 1604, had said that it should be undertaken 'by the best learned men in both the Universities, after them to be reviewed by the Bishops and the chief learned of the Church; from them to be presented to the Privy Council; and lastly to be ratified by his Royal authority'. Mention may be made of three of those who took leading parts in the work.

Of *Lancelot Andrewes*, who headed the Westminster group of ten, and who himself was Dean of Westminster before becoming Bishop of Chichester, of Ely, and lastly of Winchester, it was said that 'he might have been interpreter general at Babel . . . the world wanted learning to know how learned he was'. He is, of course, famous not only for his learning, but for his piety; and his works, and perhaps especially his *Private Prayers*, are a peculiarly precious part of the heritage of the Anglican, and indeed of the ecumenical, Church. T. S. Eliot, in a glowing appreciation of him,[45] spoke of him as 'one of the community of the born spiritual . . . intellect and sensibility were in harmony; and hence arise the particular qualities of his style'. The place which he occupied was 'second to none in the history of the formation of the English Church'. 'In both Hooker and Andrewes . . . we find . . . that breadth of culture, an ease with humanism and Renaissance learning, which helped to put them on terms of equality with their Continental antagonists and to elevate their Church above the position of a local heretical

[44] The list, so far as it is obtainable, is given in C. C. Butterworth, op. cit., p. 208, and in B. F. Westcott, op. cit., p. 147 ff.
[45] T. S. Eliot, *For Lancelot Andrewes, Essays on Style and Order* (Faber and Gwyer, 1928)

sect.' The influence of such a man as this was bound to permeate the work of the Committee of which he was the Chairman.

Dr. John Overall, who was Regius Professor of Theology at the University of Cambridge, 1596–1607, Master of Catharine Hall, Dean of St. Paul's Cathedral, and later (1614) Bishop of Coventry and Lichfield, then of Norwich, was also a member of the Westminster group. He was a schoolfellow and later college friend of John Boys, and a member of the Committee which sat at Cambridge. It is recorded of the latter that 'he abode', as the guest of St. John's College, 'all the week till Saturday night, and then went home to discharge his cure; returning thence on Monday morning'. This he did for four years. Unhappy parish!

To *Dr. John Reynolds*, President of Corpus Christi College, Oxford, and great Puritan leader, goes the credit of having been the one at the Hampton Court Conference to 'move his Majesty, that there might be a new translation of the Bible'. He cited certain passages where the translation was 'corrupt and not answerable to the truth of the Original'. Thus did his suggestion, introduced incidentally into a Conference which met to deal with the complaints of Puritan clergy especially about rites and ceremonies, give rise to that Version which is the greatest treasure in the English language.

Those who are interested in the principles on which this great work was done may be referred to the 'Preface of the Translators', written by Dr. Miles Smith. (This is to be distinguished from the rather servile dedication to the King which is to be found at the beginning of many printed copies of the Authorised Version). Here it will suffice to quote the following: 'We never thought from the beginning, that we should need to make a new Translation, nor yet to make of a bad one a good one . . . but to make a good one better, or out of many good ones, one principal good one, not justly to be excepted against; that hath been our endeavour, that our mark.'

As we try to assess the reasons for the nobility of a version which has worn supremely well for over three and a half centuries, we may attribute its supremacy to a consensus of causes, not least of which is the piety, as well as the intellectual brilliance, of those who were

responsible for its production. 'There were many chosen,' says the
Preface, 'that were greater in other men's eyes than in their own,
and that sought the truth rather than their own praise.' Further,
we must remember the age in which they lived. It was the age of
Shakespeare, Spenser, Hooker, Bacon, Marlowe, and other literary
giants. The influence of such an age is seen in the strong simplicity
of the language which those responsible for the 1611 Version used.
What can compare with such passages as these: 'The flowers
appear on the earth; the time of the singing of birds is come, and
the voice of the turtle is heard in our land',[46] or 'Thus will I bless
thee while I live: I will lift up my hands in thy name',[47] or 'Her
ways are ways of pleasantness, and all her paths are peace',[48] or
'The Son of Man is come to seek and to save that which was lost',[49]
or again 'Behold what manner of love the Father hath bestowed
upon us, that we should be called the sons of God'?[50]

It is the greatness of simplicity which characterises the Authorised
Version. No wonder that it has powerfully gripped the imagination
and the affection of the English-speaking peoples.[51]

Shelley once wrote of

> Deathless minds which leave where they have past
> A path of light.[52]

It is a fair description of those whose lives and work we have
glanced at in this chapter. 'Deathless minds'—John Wycliffe,
John Purvey, Nicholas Hereford, William Tyndale, Miles Coverdale, Desiderius Erasmus, John Rogers, Lancelot Andrewes, John
Overall, John Reynolds and others in that galaxy of scholars who
gave us the Authorised Version of 1611—truly they left 'a path of
light'. It was the light which shone from the Bible given to the

[46] S. of S. 2:12
[47] Ps. 63:4
[48] Prov. 3:17
[49] Luke 19:10
[50] 1 John 3:1
[51] T. R. Henn, in his *The Bible as Literature* (Lutterworth, 1970), has a
valuable chapter on 'The Forge of Style', pp. 46 ff., in which he analyses
the styles of various versions such as those of Wycliffe, Tyndale, Coverdale,
King James and some modern ones.
[52] *The Revolt of Islam*, Canto II, 20

people in a language which they could understand. These translations illustrate well the dictum of Miles Coverdale: 'Sure I am that there cometh more knowledge and understanding of the scripture by their sundry translations than by all the glosses of our sophistical doctors.'

5

A Century of Advance (1870-1970)

In 1870, work was begun on the Revised Version of the Bible. In 1970, the complete New English Bible was published. The century between these two important dates has been one of great advance, in biblical scholarship, in experimentation in translation, in production.

It was preceded by a drab period. Nor is this altogether surprising. The influence of the 1611 Version was so immense, with its direct indebtedness to the three giants, Wycliffe, Tyndale and Coverdale, and the language of the period was so superb that any later attempts tended to suffer by comparison. We have noticed the majestic simplicity of the Authorised Version. Eighteenth century attempts at translation only serve to underline this by their prolixity and floridity. Thus, there was published in 1729 anonymously (though the writer is known; his name was Mace) *The New Testament in Greek and English . . . corrected from the Authority of the most Authentic Manuscripts.* Three examples will show how far Mace fell from the example set in 1611. In the Authorised Version Luke 17:27 runs: 'They did eat, they drank, they married wives, they were given in marriage.' Mace reads: 'Eating and drinking, marriages and matches, was the business.' In the Authorised Version James 2:3 runs: '[if] ye have respect to him that weareth the gay clothing, and say unto him, Sit thou here in a good place . . .' Mace reads: 'If you should respectfully say to the suit of fine cloths, sit you there, that's for quality . . .' In the Authorised Version, James 3:5 and 6 runs: '. . . the tongue is a little member, and boasteth great things. Behold how great a matter a little fire kindleth! And the tongue is a fire, a world of iniquity: so is the tongue among our members, that it defileth the whole body, and setteth on fire the course of nature; and it is set on fire of hell.' Mace reads: 'The tongue is but a small part of the body, yet how

67

grand are its pretensions! a spark of fire! What quantities of timber will it blow into a flame? The tongue is a brand that sets the world in a combustion: it is but one of the numerous organs of the body, yet it can blast whole assemblies: tipp'd with infernal sulphur it sets the whole train of life in a blaze.'

Anthony Purver's version of 1764 does no better. The lovely words of the Song of Solomon[1] quoted in the last chapter are spoilt, almost to the point of the ludicrous: 'Earth's Lap displays her infant Flowers, the warbling Spring is welcomed in, and hark how the Turtle-dove coos in our Clime.' It is all very depressing.

Between 1611 and 1881 there were other translations of parts of the Bible, but it would not be unfair to say that none of them has made any great or permanent mark on the record. The event of real importance in these two hundred and seventy years was the publication of the Revised Version. Like the Authorised Version, it was the work of committees—three in the case of the Revised Version as compared with six in the case of the Authorised. As the members of the Joint Committee of the New English Bible were to do in the following century, the twenty-seven members of the New Testament Revision Committee met in the Jerusalem Chamber of Westminster Abbey. They began their work, as we have seen, in June 1870, finished it in 1880, and it was published in 1881. The Old Testament Committee met in the Westminster Chapter Library, the thirty-seven members beginning, like their New Testament brethren, in 1870 but spending fourteen years on the task, the results of their work being published in 1885. The Apocrypha Committee split its work up between its members who met in London, Westminster and Cambridge and completed its work in 1895.

As in the case of the Authorised Version, the committees which did the work were composed of men of great distinction and learning, representative of biblical scholarship at its best in England, Scotland, Ireland and America.[2] Certainly the time was ripe for a

[1] S. of S. 2:12
[2] For particulars of the personnel, which included B. F. Westcott and F. J. A. Hort, see Westcott, op. cit., p. 343 ff. It is of interest that the Reverend (later Professor) S. R. Driver was a member of the Old Testa-

revision. Many changes had taken place in the English language in the course of nearly three hundred years. Further, immense strides had been made in exegetical and philological work since the seventeenth century. There searches of the great Cambridge trio, Westcott, Lightfoot and Hort alone mark an epoch. If, as we look back over the years which separate our own times from those of the Revised Version, we feel how small an impact the Revised Version has made on the English people as compared with that made by the Authorised Version, that fact is less due to any faults in the later version than to the amazing hold that the Authorised Version had obtained and still maintains on the affections of our race. The Revised Version, while not possessing the literary qualities which made the Authorised Version so outstanding, yet was more accurate and consistent in its details, and more faithful in its adherence to scientific principles. It was precisely what its title indicates—not a new translation of the original languages but a revision of the Authorised Version.

We have said that the time was ripe for a revision of the Bible. That is quite true when we consider the period that had elapsed since anything had been done on a national scale. Yet there is a sense in which it would be true to say that the Revised Version was made some fifty years too soon. The closing decade or so of the nineteenth century and the opening two or three decades of the twentieth century were years of the utmost importance in the studies which bear on biblical scholarship. Progress was made in those decades which tended to out-date work done previously. A very few men had been able dimly to foresee an irruption of new knowledge. As far back as 1863 Professor (afterwards Bishop) J. B. Lightfoot had said in a lecture, 'You are not to suppose that the word [some New Testament word which had its only classical authority in Herodotus] had fallen out of use in the interval, only that it had not been used in the books which remain to us: probably it had been part of the common speech all along. I will go further,

----

ment Committee. His son Professor (later Sir Godfrey) Driver took a leading part in the production of the New English Bible. Thus father and son spanned nearly a century in the work of the revision of the English Bible.

and say that if we could only recover letters that ordinary people wrote to each other without any thought of being literary, we should have the greatest possible help for the understanding of the language of the New Testament generally.'[3] That was scholarly prevision at its best. But even by 1881 the full force of the rising tide of new knowledge had not been felt, and was not to be felt yet for some time.

Shortly after the Revised Version came out, the dry sands of the Near East, and especially of Egypt, threw up thousands upon thousands of ostraca (old pieces of broken pots and vessels) and papyri (sheets, some fairly large and others no more than little scraps, of papyrus reeds glued together, rubbed smooth with pumice, and used as we should use bits of paper). On these ostraca and papyri were written in the Greek of the street, the market-place and the home, all kinds of things, for example, lists of names or articles, and messages of all sorts. (One such, in atrocious Greek, is from a schoolboy asking his father for money; another is from a husband on military service, writing to his wife who is expecting the birth of their child. 'If it is a boy,' he writes, 'well and good; if it is a girl, cast it out.') At first sight one would not think that such discoveries would have much bearing on biblical scholarship. As a matter of fact, they were of the greatest importance. For, as these little scraps of writing were gathered together, deciphered, and compared with the Greek in which the New Testament was written, it became clear that the New Testament documents, so far from being written (as many had previously thought) in a kind of special 'language of the Holy Ghost', were, as a matter of fact, written in the ordinary language used by the people of the first century Graeco–Roman world. True, the themes with which the documents dealt had an ennobling effect on the language and, as it were, lifted it out of the street on to a higher plane. True, the Hebraic thought of many of the writers and the use of the Greek Version of the Old Testament, the Septuagint, influenced the style of the Greek. True, some of the writers of the New Testament were men of culture and great literary skill—St. Luke especially, and

[3] Quoted by Professor G. Milligan in *Here and There among the Papyri* (Hodder and Stoughton, 1923), pp. 61–62

the unknown author of the Epistle to the Hebrews. But *basically* the language was that of the lingua franca which was the chief means of intercourse among the peoples of the Mediterranean world of the time of Christ. Many of the discoveries were in themselves of no importance. (For example, the Authorised Version of Luke 15:13, makes the Prodigal son 'gather all together' before he goes into the far country. The papyri have shown that the verb can mean 'realise goods into ready cash'. This is precisely what he needed if he was to 'have a good time'!) But taken together, they opened up something of a new epoch in New Testament textual study.

All this was 'around the corner' when the revisers got busy with their work. But the time had not arrived when such discoveries could be used and incorporated in the work of revision. The result was the production of a volume which, while it was to be used, especially by students, for several decades to come, yet fell disappointingly short of what it might have been had it appeared early in the twentieth century instead of late in the nineteenth.

The terms of reference under which the committees worked were cautious. 'We do not contemplate any new translation of the Bible,' the committees of the Canterbury Convocation had said, 'or any alteration of the language, except when in the judgement of the most competent scholars such change is necessary.' When such changes were made, 'the style of the language employed in the existing version' (i.e. the Authorised Version) was to 'be closely followed'. If the revision proved sometimes to be somewhat pedantic (partly as a result of the attempt always to translate a Greek word by the same English word wherever it occurred); and if the New Testament part of it leaned too heavily on the Vatican and Sinaitic codices (technically known as B and Aleph respectively) owing to the influence especially of Westcott and Hort, still the Revised Version was an immense improvement on the Authorised, especially in obscure parts of the Old Testament; in the paragraphing according to the sense of the passage; and in the marginal notes which deal with alternative renderings and variant readings. It is true that the Authorised Version was so securely established in the affections of the people that the Revised Version never dislodged it. To many then (as indeed now) the Authorised Version *was* 'the Bible'! But where a text of the Bible in English was required by students, there the Revised Version came into its own, particularly after the University Presses of Oxford and Cambridge produced an edition with marginal references, as they did in 1898.[4]

The twentieth century has been a period of intense activity in the field of biblical translation. Never before have so much knowledge and skill gone to putting into practice the Reformation principle that 'the very pure Word of God, the Holy Scriptures' be 'not bound' but set forth in such 'a Language and Order as is most easy and plain for the understanding both of the Readers and Hearers'.[5]

Only a few of the new translations can be mentioned here.[6] Among these, Dr. R. F. Weymouth's *New Testament in Modern Speech* should not go unmentioned. First published in 1902, it met a real need among students of the Bible, as is witnessed by the fact that it passed through many editions. The work of one who had been Head Master of Mill Hill School, it shows the marks of scholarship and at the same time of reverence. It is still worth referring to.

Passing by with only a mention of the translation of J. N. Darby (popular especially among the Plymouth Brethren), and *The Modern Reader's Bible* by Dr. R. G. Moulton (1907), we come to the famous and outstanding translation of Dr. James Moffatt. The production of this work (New Testament 1913, Old Testament 1924, the whole Bible finally revised in 1935) was a landmark in the story of modern biblical translations. Dr. Moffatt was a biblical theologian and Church historian of international reputation. In his

[4] For an account of the birth of the Revised Version, an assessment of some of the main scholars concerned in its production, and an estimate of the reception accorded to it, see Owen Chadwick, *The Victorian Church* (A. and C. Black, 1970), part II, p. 44 ff.

[5] The Original Preface to the *Book of Common Prayer* (1549) altered in 1552 and 1662. Concerning the Service of the Church.

[6] For a more complete treatment of the subject see E. H. Robertson, *The New Translations of the Bible* (S.C.M. Press, *Studies in Ministry and Worship* No. 12, 1959). See also L. A. Weigle in *The Cambridge History of the Bible: The West from the Reformation to the Present Day* (Cambridge University Press, 1963), pp. 361–82.

translation, he tried to break away from old styles of translation, and to give us the biblical books in the idiom of modern English. Moreover, he tried to incorporate, in so far as was possible, some of the results of modern source criticism. Very often he did not hesitate to re-arrange the order of the text in order to show how, in his opinion, such a re-arrangement would improve the sense. It may be that to some this procedure is a source of annoyance; that to others the constant recurrence of 'the Eternal' for the divine Name is unsatisfactory; that in public the version fails to 'read' anything like as well as does the melodious Authorised Version. (Who, for example, would venture to read in public Job's lament over the day of his birth, in chapter 3:3, 'Perish . . . the night that said, "It's a boy"'?) Granted all this, it remains true that Moffatt's version succeeded—and still succeeds—in bringing the Bible alive to those who had at least been in danger of being lulled to sleep by the cadences of 1611. Moffatt is almost merciless in the way he brings out the passion of indignation of prophet and psalmist, or the fierce episodes of Israelite history. There is no doubt that subsequent versions have improved on Moffatt's work. But the credit of being something of a pioneer in this field rests with this great Scotsman.

On the other side of the Atlantic, Professor Edgar Goodspeed produced his American translation of the New Testament (1923), the Old Testament work being handled by a team of scholars under the guidance of Professor J. M. Powis Smith (1927). Goodspeed was anxious that the people of his country should possess a modern translation of their own, which incorporated recent finds of scholarship, including those which derived from the ostraca and papyri to which reference has already been made. Further, as in Moffatt's translation, poetry was printed in verse form—an immense advantage over the old method of printing the Bible.

The English-speaking world is indebted to the committee of thirty-two American scholars who in 1946 put out the Revised Standard Version of the New Testament. The whole Bible appeared in 1952. It is read in many British homes and churches, the 'Americanisms' being sufficiently rare to annoy only the most fastidious. The language is modern but dignified, and reads more easily in public than do some of the more radical translations. The Version can be criticised for being over-cautious in retaining words like 'pate' and 'man-child'. But the omission of 'thee', 'thou', 'thine' in ordinary speech, the printing of the poetic passages in such a way that they can be seen as poetry, the breaking up into short sentences of the long Pauline ones—all these things are great gains, as is the incorporation of certain emendations of the text which have generally commended themselves to scholars. Basing their work on the American Standard Version of 1901, the committee thoroughly revised it, and embodied the results of modern scholarship, preserving 'those qualities which have given to the King James Version a supreme place in English literature'.

The year 1949 saw the publication of Ronald Knox's translation of the Old and New Testaments, 'from the Latin Vulgate at the request of the Cardinal Archbishop of Westminster—for private use only'. It was an astonishing achievement, including as it did the Apocrypha and, just for good value, two translations of the Psalms! Knox's biographer[7] makes it clear how big a place the task occupied in the translator's life. The disadvantage of a translation from the Vulgate is, in part, offset by the notes which make it abundantly clear that Knox kept a very careful eye on the original languages. The Latin form of the proper names (Neomi for Naomi, and Booz for Boaz) may be annoying to non-Roman Catholic readers. But there is a dignity and power of style about Knox's translation which make it worthy of constant reference.

The publication of J. B. Phillips's *Letters to Young Churches*, with an introduction by C. S. Lewis (1947), was an exciting event. It was followed by *The Gospels in Modern English* (1952), by *The Young Church in Action* (The Acts of the Apostles, 1955), and by *The Book of Revelation* (1957). The whole *New Testament in Modern English* appeared in 1958. This was the work of an Anglican clergyman who was convinced that the New Testament has a living message for the people of today, but that the message is dimmed and dulled by the kind of English in which they are compelled to read it. His work is not by any means a word-for-word translation. Nor is it wholly a paraphrase. Professor F. F. Bruce

[7] Evelyn Waugh, *Ronald Knox* (Chapman and Hall, 1959)

says that 'what he gives us is a meaning-for-meaning translation'.[8] It has had a phenomenal success on both sides of the Atlantic, and has succeeded in tearing aside for multitudes the veil that has hidden from them the meaning of the New Testament books. The message has become 'contemporaneous'.

Readers of *English Translators and Translations*[9] will be familiar with the distinguished work of Dr. E. V. Rieu in the realm of the translation of the classics. In 1952 he produced in the Penguin Classics a translation of *The Four Gospels*, with an admirable introduction. This was followed in the same series by a translation of the *Acts of the Apostles*, by his son C. H. Rieu (1957).

The publication of the *New English Bible* in 1970 was a major event, in the world of scholarship, of printing, and of ecumenical co-operation. The New Testament had been published in 1961 and had had a great reception. The year 1970 saw the completion of the work with the issuing of the Old Testament and Apocrypha together with a (slight) revision of the New Testament. The story of this work, which from its conception to its publication took some twenty-four years, has been told in detail by Geoffrey Hunt who was a member of the staff of the Oxford University Press during the whole time that the New English Bible was in preparation.[10] Here an outline of the story must suffice.

The purpose of the enterprise was unashamedly evangelistic and educational. It was increasingly recognised by church leaders after the end of the Second World War that the language of the Authorised and Revised Versions, for all its beauty, was a very real hindrance to the understanding of its message by many people. Macaulay, in a famous sentence, had said of the Authorised Ver-

[8] F. F. Bruce, *The English Bible: A History of Translations from the Earliest English Versions to the New English Bible* (Lutterworth, 1961; revised edn 1970), p. 214

[9] J. M. Cohen, *English Translators and Translations*, no. 142 in the series *Writers and their Work* published for the British Council and the National Book League by Longmans, Green

[10] Geoffrey Hunt, *About the New English Bible* (Oxford University Press, Cambridge University Press, 1970). The story is more briefly told in the *Handbook to the New English Bible*, published by the same University Presses, 1970

sion that it was 'a book which, if everything else in our language should perish, would alone suffice to show the whole extent of its beauty and power'. That was a high tribute and we have already alluded to it.[11] But the primary purpose of the Bible is not to exhibit linguistic beauty, though, if that can be achieved, it is much to be desired. The Bible is not simply 'designed to be read as literature'. When Jeremiah wrote, 'Do not my words scorch like fire? says the Lord. Are they not like a hammer that splinters rock?', he was, of course, referring to the spoken word of God which came to the people through his agency.[12] But it is also true of the word of God that comes to men through the Scriptures. 'Fire', 'hammer'— these are rough, tough metaphors. Fire burns, and obliterates, and melts, and purges, and unites what otherwise cannot be united (as in the soldering of metals). And a hammer breaks, splits asunder, rends in pieces. So it is when God speaks his word to men—directly through human agency or through the Bible. There is a burning and a rending, and men find that the things they most loved are shattered and gone. The sin that so easily besets them is purged, and the disunion which hitherto they had so complacently tolerated is soldered into God's unity. The rock of their hard hearts and of their ecclesiastical respectability is broken in pieces.

Such is the nature of the word that comes to men from God through the Bible. It is, therefore, of first importance that nothing should impede its impact, reduce its heat, soften its hammer-blow. It was a deep concern to see that this should not happen which led to the concept of a new translation.

A new translation—totally new—not a revision of an old one; a translation which would incorporate the findings of the most recent scholarship (including, for example, the evidence produced by the Dead Sea scrolls); a translation which would have an authority greater than that of any one scholar, be he a Moffatt or a Knox— all this was looked for. The level of scholarship was guaranteed by the fact that the panels which did the work included some of the best Hebrew, Greek and English scholars living in the United Kingdom. Its 'authority' was guaranteed by the fact that those who

[11] *vide supra*, p. 63
[12] Jer. 23:29 N.E.B.

did the work, and those who supervised its progress in the Joint Committee, were representative of the main strands of non-Roman churchmanship—it was only towards the end of the work that Roman Catholic representatives joined the Joint Committee as observers. The work of the panels—Old Testament, New Testament and Apocrypha—was carefully considered by the Literary Panel, the members of which 'scrutinised it . . . verse by verse, sentence by sentence, and took pains to secure as best they could the tone and level of language appropriate to the different kinds of writing to be found in the Bible, whether narrative, familiar discourse, argument, law, rhetoric or poetry'.[13] Though the primary purpose of the translation was not to provide a work for reading in public, it is likely that in fact its English will prove to be good enough in experience for that purpose and not only for private study.

Those who want to appreciate the work done by the four panels and the kind of problems that faced them would do well to read an admirable essay by Professor Basil Willey, entitled 'On Translating the Bible into Modern English'.[14] He was for eighteen years a member of the panel of Literary Advisers. He begins with a tribute to 'the extraordinary hold exerted by this numinous book'—he is referring to the Authorised Version—'over the hearts and minds of Englishmen and (later) of all English-speaking peoples'. He proceeds to justify the production of an entirely new translation on grounds of the need to avail ourselves of new scholarship, and also of the *un*familiarity of many so-called 'educated' people today with the Authorised Version: 'The new masses have not read or heard the Bible at their mother's knee.' He concludes 'that the N.E.B. New Testament was an outstanding achievement'.

Perhaps the most interesting pages of Basil Willey's essay are those in which he illustrates the kind of difficulties faced by the Literary Panel at a typical Old Testament session as the members tested 'the diction, tone, euphony and rhythms', and saw to it that

[13] Preface to the *New English Bible,* p. vi

[14] *Essays and Studies 1970,* being volume 23 of the new series of essays and studies collected for the English Association by A. R. Humphreys (John Murray, 1970)

they were as fitting as possible to the kind of book in question. I know no other record of the work of the long years spent in the production of the N.E.B. which so vividly describes the approach of the members of the panel to the problems which confronted them. Thus, to take only one example: 'Tell it not in Gath'[15] is not modern English. But this is a poetic passage, and, in addition, the phrase has become so familiar as to be an English saying known to all educated people (even if they could not all give the context!). 'Do not tell it in Gath' is banal. What were the members of the panel to do? They retained the older form. Were they right? Basil Willey thinks so. Many would agree with him. But the debate which preceded this decision was typical of a thousand others.

Though the names of those responsible for the work are not printed in the Preface to the N.E.B.—they are to be found in Hunt's book already referred to[16]—it would hardly be an exaggeration to say that the presiding genius from start to finish was Professor C. H. Dodd, whose biblical scholarship and sensitiveness to the nuances of theology and language are known all over the world. Professor (later Sir) Godfrey Driver and Professor W. D. McHardy as Convenors of the Old Testament and Apocrypha Panels respectively carried, with Professor Dodd, the heaviest part of the load, particularly in the later years of the work. It was a happy thing that Professor J. K. S. Reid, of the Church of Scotland, was throughout the operation its Secretary, for the original suggestion 'that a translation of the Bible be made in the language of the present day' emanated from the General Assembly of the Church of Scotland held in May 1946.

The Presses of the Universities of Oxford and Cambridge have given great care to the presentation to the reader of the work that the scholars produced. Such matters as the avoidance of double columns, the allocation to the margin of verse numbers, the printing of poetry in verse form as distinct from prose in paragraphs—all these things and a dozen others have led to the production of a book which is easy to read and to handle. The sale of the first edition of the New Testament had reached about seven million copies

[15] 2 Sam. 1:20
[16] Geoffrey Hunt, op. cit., pp. 78–82

by the time its revision appeared, and that of the complete Bible was reckoned at some two million by October 1970.

Mention must be made of two more very recent translations of the New Testament. *Good News for Modern Man: the New Testament in Today's English Version* was first published by the American Bible Society in 1966 in New York. The basic text was translated by Dr. Robert G. Bratcher, a translations consultant of the American Bible Society. The Greek text used by him was that prepared by an international committee of New Testament scholars sponsored by several member societies of the United Bible Societies. The translation is, in the words of the Preface, an attempt 'to follow, in this century, the example set by the authors of the New Testament books who, for the most part, wrote in the standard, or common, form of the Greek language used throughout the Roman Empire. As much as possible, words and forms of English not in current use have been avoided . . .' In four years, twenty-five million copies have been published, and sales are accelerating. It is proving to be a translation with a peculiar ability to communicate truth; this is facilitated by the line drawings of Annie Vallotton, to which reference is made elsewhere in this book.[17]

The Living New Testament is more than a translation. It is a paraphrase; and the purpose of a paraphrase is, in the words of the Preface, 'to say as exactly as possible what the New Testament writer meant, and to say it simply, adding words where necessary for greater accuracy . . .' That there are dangers as well as values in paraphrases is admitted in the Preface, and no one scholar will agree with all the interpretations which this particular paraphrase necessarily imports into the translation. But that there is need for such a work is apparent, and the printing in 1969 by Hodder and Stoughton of an edition of this American work designed for British readers is to be welcomed. The publication of the complete *Living Bible* at about the same time as the appearance of this book is awaited with interest.

In these last two chapters, it has only been possible to touch on some of the main translations which have been made between the

[17] *vide infra*, pp. 104–5

time of John Wycliffe and our own. Even so, the story is impressive enough. Those who want to have more detail should consult the *Historical Catalogue of Printed Editions of the English Bible 1525–1961*, revised and expanded from the edition of T. H. Darlow and H. F. Moule, 1903, by A. S. Herbert, Professor of Old Testament Literature and Religion, Selly Oak Colleges, Birmingham.[18] It is a work of great erudition, beginning with Tyndale's work and going down to the N.E.B. New Testament. As the opening sentence of Professor Herbert's *Introduction* well says: 'Any history of the English Printed Bible, even an historical catalogue, might well have as a sub-title, "The Word of God is not fettered" (2 Timothy 2:9 R.S.V.).'

[18] Published by the British and Foreign Bible Society, 1968; American Bible Society, 1968

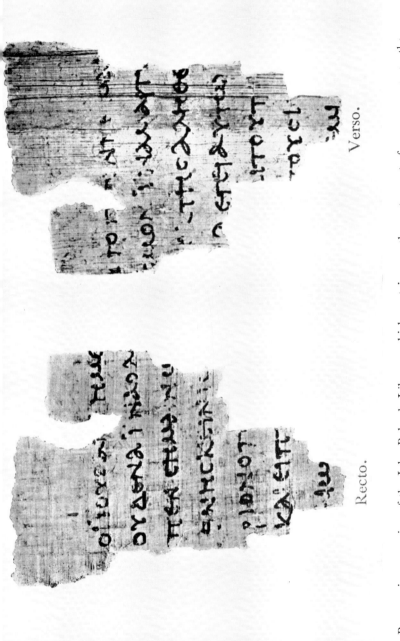

Verso.

Recto.

Papyrus in possession of the John Rylands Library, which contains, on the recto, part of verses 31–33, on the verso, part of verses 37–38, of chapter 18 of St John's Gospel. First half of the second century.

William Tyndale (1494–1536). A pioneer in the translation of the
Scriptures into the English language. Statue in the Victoria Embankment
Gardens, London

The directors of the New English Bible (from left) the Rev. Dr C. H. Dodd, CH, Professor Sir Godfrey Driver, and the Rev. Professor W. D. McHardy, looking at a printed sheet of the Old Testament in the University Press, Oxford

KEY

1 The Ven. C. J. Stranks (Church of England)
2 The Rev. Princ. C. L. Mitton (Methodist Church)
3 The Rev. Professor W. D. McHardy, Deputy Director
4 Professor Sir Godfrey Driver, Joint Director
5 The Rev. Dr C. H. Dodd, CH, Joint Director
6 The Most Rev. and Rt Hon. the Lord Archbishop of York, Chairman
7 The Rev. Professor J. K. S. Reid, Secretary
8 Miss Phoebe Allen, secretariat
9 Mr R. W. David (Cambridge University Press)
10 Mr C. F. Eccleshare (Cambridge University Press)
11 Mr John Brown (Oxford University Press)
12 Mr C. H. Roberts (Oxford University Press)
13 The Rev. J. C. O'Neill (Presbyterian Church of England)
14 The Rev. Thomas Hanlon (Roman Catholic Observer)
15 The Rt Rev. the Lord Bishop of Winchester (Church of England)
16 The Rev. H. K. Moulton (British and Foreign Bible Society)
17 Dr E. A. Payne, CH (Baptist Union)
18 The Rev. Professor Kenneth Grayston (Methodist Church)
19 Dr George Boobyer (Society of Friends)
20 The Rev. Professor J. L. M. Haire (Churches in Ireland)
21 The Rev. R. L. Child (Baptist Union)
22 The Rev. D. E. Nineham (Church of England)
23 The Rev. Professor N. W. Porteous (Church of Scotland)

The last meeting of the Joint Committee of sponsoring Churches before publication of the complete New English Bible. In the Jerusalem Chamber at Westminster Abbey

A group of students leaving a classroom after a lecture at the Africa Literature Centre, Kitwe, Zambia

A stop-over for the Bookvan at a hospital in Zambia

The Dag Hammarskjöld Memorial Library at the Mindolo Ecumenical Centre, Zambia, of which the African Literature Centre is a part.

Printing 'New Day', a Christian Newspaper, Uganda

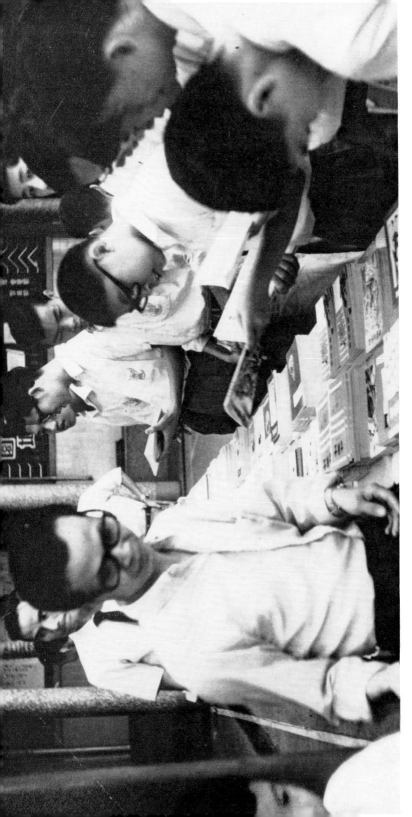

Christian books find interested readers amongst Hong Kong schoolboys

6

'Into All the World'

So far in this book we have looked at the events which constituted 'the greatest drama ever staged', and the ways in which, during the early years of the Church's history, expression was given to the mighty acts of God in Christ. We have seen how it became possible for the Church to go on its missionary errand to the world with a book in its hand, a book in two parts, Old Testament and New. We have watched, very briefly, the translation of that book in the early centuries into the major languages of the Mediterranean basin and in greater detail and in later centuries, into the English tongue during its development over a very long period up to the present day. It is a long and complicated and noble story, and a wide variety of people—scholars, preachers, martyrs—makes up its *dramatis personae*.

An entirely new epoch in the story of the spread of the Bible began with the missionary expansion of the Church at the end of the eighteenth century and the beginning of the nineteenth.

It is quite clear that, towards the end of the fifteenth century, when the great discoveries of new lands which we associate with such names as Diaz and Columbus were being made, the Roman Catholic Church saw to it that the Christian Faith was firmly planted in those lands. So far as the Roman Catholic Church was concerned, the ensuing centuries were years of vast missionary expansion. Alas, it was not so with the churches of the Reformation tradition. The reasons for this lack of missionary vision have been variously estimated. No doubt they were in large part due to the failure of such leading Reformers as Luther and Calvin to see the missionary obligations of their theology. Dr. Leslie Davison follows William R. Hogg in the three main reasons he gives for this failure. Hogg points out that the Protestant repudiation of the Papacy and its claim to world sovereignty removed the main motive of mission as the sixteenth century understood it. Similarly the Protestant abolition of the religious orders eliminated the chief source of trained missionary personnel and there was as yet no substitute. Thirdly both Catholics and Protestants were afraid of freelance lay evangelism, such as that fostered by the Anabaptists whom both sides savagely repressed. So in Protestant lands there was no concern for mission overseas.[1] It is a sad story.

As the end of the eighteenth century gave way to the beginning of the nineteenth, however, a period of unparalleled missionary expansion set in. It might well have been otherwise. England had enough to keep her busy. She had been at war with France since 1793, with but little respite. In 1804, the year when the British and Foreign Bible Society was founded, the country was more exposed to the dangers of invasion than in any year before 1940. Napoleon was planning to carry 100,000 troops across the Channel. 'Eight hours of darkness which favour us,' he said, 'would decide the fate of the universe.' Declared Emperor of the French in May 1804, it was his ambition to include England in his Empire. The British might have been forgiven if they had pleaded preoccupation with their own concerns and had postponed any new work abroad. But as a matter of fact, this proved to be the time in England's history when men of vision were more alert to the divine commission to preach the Gospel to all nations than they had ever been in their long history.

In 1792 William Carey urged his friends to form the Baptist Missionary Society. In 1795 the London Missionary Society was founded. In 1799 the Church Missionary Society (or, to give it its original title, the Society for Missions in Africa and the East) began work in Africa. True, its beginnings were small (it sent out five missionaries in the first ten years of its existence) and its first missionaries were Germans, but they were soon joined by men and women from England, and a pioneer work of great proportions was born. There is something deeply moving about the way in which men and women gave themselves to the missionary cause. Many were martyred. Many others lost their lives in conditions of

[1] *Sender and Sent*, p. 68

extreme heat or cold and as the result of diseases for which at that time there was no known cure. At home, the work of organising missionary outreach went ahead, and large sums of money were given to the prosecution of the task.

The Society for Promoting Christian Knowledge had been founded as much as a century before the Church Missionary Society. G. M. Trevelyan notes of S.P.C.K. (founded 1698) 'and its off-shoot, the Society for the Propagation of the Gospel in Foreign Parts' (founded 1701), with their 'chief object' of diffusing the Bible and other religious literature, that 'these activities betokened an instinctive movement of the English religious world to get away, on one side at least, from the denominational and political feuds in which it was entangled, into a field of broader vision, where zeal might produce something better than hate'.[2] It was a noble work. But the S.P.C.K. could meet only a fraction of the demand for Bibles, or Testaments. A new Society was needed. In the midst of the turmoil of war and of threatened invasion that Society was born—on March 7th, 1804.

The story of the birth and expansion of the British and Foreign Bible Society has often been told—officially in the great *History of the Bible Society 1804-1904*, by William Canton[3] and in *The History of the British and Foreign Bible Society 1905-1954*, by James Moulton Roe.[4] Not the least valuable part of Roe's book is his Introduction of twenty-four pages, in which he gives a resumé of the first hundred years for those who have not the time or inclination to work through Canton's five substantial volumes. It is a fascinating story.

If the details of the episode of Mary Jones's twenty-eight mile walk to spend her entire savings on the purchase of a Bible have 'since elevated it to a position in which its symbolic value somewhat exceeds its historical significance' (to use Mr. Roe's cautious words[5]), we cannot over-estimate the importance of the meeting of the Religious Tract Society on December 7th, 1802 in London. At

[2] *English Social History*, p. 329
[3] Five volumes, 1904–10
[4] J. M. Roe, *The History of the British and Foreign Bible Society, 1905–1954* (B.F.B.S., 1965)
[5] op. cit., p. 2

this meeting the Reverend Thomas Charles spoke of the need of the people of Wales for the Bible. 'Surely,' he said, 'a Society might be formed for the purpose. But if for Wales, why not for the Kingdom? Why not for the world?' Formed it was in February 1804 at a meeting at the London Tavern in Bishopsgate, its General Committee consisting entirely of laymen, fifteen of them Anglicans, fifteen members of the Free Churches, and six 'foreigners resident in or near London'. So began a work which was soon to become world-wide in its outreach and a society which was to be the 'parent' of a family of societies with an identical aim, later to be united under the auspices of the United Bible Societies.[6]

As the nineteenth century passed into the twentieth and as the twentieth century progressed, men were beginning to think globally in a way not previously possible. The idea of a British Empire (later a Commonwealth of Nations), composed of people of many nationalities and colours and religions, but with a common loyalty which bound them together—this helped towards a global view. Science lent a mighty hand to the concept—for as science advanced, the world shrank; travel became ever more rapid and easy; intercourse between nations ever more frequent; cross-fertilisation of ideas ever more fruitful. Later, the world was to see the emergence of the League of Nations, then of the United Nations Organisation. The physical ills which flesh was heir to demanded a World Health Organisation. World conferences of experts in the different fields of human endeavour became more and more the order of the day. 'Workers of the *world*, unite!' Students of the world joined forces; and Christian students in the closing decades of the nineteenth century and the opening decades of the twentieth found themselves conferring, planning and organising more and more on an international basis.

It was natural and right that, in a world which thought increasingly in global terms, the Church should also do so. As the world shrank, as the missionary task expanded, the tragedy of the Church's disunity became all the more glaringly obvious in all its sinfulness. It is perhaps impossible to give an exact date to the beginning of what we now call the ecumenical movement. But there

[6] *vide infra*, p. 88 ff

need be little cause for disagreement if we say that its watershed can be traced to the great Conference held in Edinburgh in June 1910. Some twelve hundred delegates, representative of many Christian bodies and some one hundred and sixty Missionary Societies or Boards, took part. John R. Mott was chairman of the committee which called the conference and J. H. Oldham its secretary. Young William Temple was present as a guest and as one of the stewards organised by the Student Christian Movement. A new day in inter-church relationships had begun.

But there were antecedents to Edinburgh 1910, the importance of which can rightly be estimated only in the light cast on them by the passage of later years. Well before 1910 there had been inter-denominational co-operation on the part of those who worked in such movements as the Young Men's Christian Association (founded in 1844 by George Williams) and the Young Women's Christian Association (founded in 1855 by Miss Robarts and Lady Kinnaird). Among such pioneering movements the British and Foreign Bible Society (and the American Bible Society and similar Societies abroad) hold a place of high honour. Here denominational barriers were at their lowest—though tensions were sometimes to be found!—as men joined hands in a common purpose to translate and disseminate the Bible wherever men could read.

It may justly be claimed that the Bible Society movement was in a very real sense a forerunner of the ecumenical movement, and without it the birth-pangs of the ecumenical movement would have been infinitely more painful than they were. Friendships had been formed in the Bible Society movement which were to continue and to fructify in wider spheres. Possibilities of co-operation had been glimpsed in Bible Society work which were to find even fuller out-lets in the movement which would see such conferences as those of Jerusalem in 1928, of Madras in 1938 and so on down to that of New Delhi in 1961, Mexico in 1963, and Uppsala in 1968. The Bible Society movement had been a kind of John the Baptist 'preparing the way' of the ecumenical movement, and many were the crooked places that were made straight as it pursued its work.

Further, it must be remembered that it was the vision of world evangelisation which gave to the ecumenical movement its thrust and its passion. The motto 'The evangelisation of the world in this generation'—a motto greatly loved by such leaders as John R. Mott and Robert P. Wilder—may be criticised by a later generation as altogether too facile, too utopian in its outlook. It was fashioned in days before the two world wars, when it was easier to think of the kingdom of God as nearing its fulfilment, when the sinister forces at work in mankind had hardly been assessed for what they were. Perhaps the movement that loved that motto was infected by the over-hopeful spirit of the age,

> God's in his heaven,
> All's right with the world.

But when all has been said, it must be repeated that the passion for world evangelism was that which gave thrust to ecumenism. And we who are still committed to that movement should ask ourselves whether it is likely to survive—indeed whether its survival is to be desired—if that passion is damped down or snuffed out.

Behind this passion for evangelism, at once its source and its stay, was the Bible.

During these decades of global thinking, of international and ecumenical conference and action, there grew up a series of national Bible Societies. For a long time they worked largely in independence of one another. But the time came when they began to see the need for far closer consultation and co-operation than had hitherto obtained.

The British and Foreign Bible Society, being located at the centre of the powerful British Empire, carried by far the largest part of the work, and along with the National Bible Society of Scotland was able to extend its activities which developed very widely within the Empire. The work of the American Bible Society, like the United States of America itself, has increased in scope and extent over the last hundred years, and has reached unparalleled dimensions in the last quarter of a century. Today its resources amount to approximately half of those of all the other Bible Societies put together. Apart from the work of the Netherlands

Bible Society and the publication in Germany of one or two 'missionary editions', the European Societies of the Continent limited their services and interest to the supply of Scriptures to their home constituency.

After the Second World War, the Bible Societies had to revise their outlook, their policies and their practical work in more ways than one. Thus after working side by side for a number of years, recognising the value of one another's activities but carrying on without organic relationship, unrelated though each working along similar lines, the three Anglo-American Societies, at the beginning of the century, agreed to comity arrangements in various areas of the world. This was replaced from the 'thirties onwards by the setting up of Joint Agencies, administered by one of the partners but financed by two or more partners. But, parallel to administrative adjustments, the issue of a world fellowship of Bible Societies began to dawn on the minds of Bible Society leaders, the first reference to it going back to 1926 in a series of consultations held by the two main Bible Societies, the American Bible Society and the British and Foreign Bible Society. Six years later in London an important step was taken at a conference of representatives of the three Anglo-American Bible Societies: a series of agreements was passed in order to facilitate the co-ordination of efforts in overseas work, publication, prices, and editorial policies. But still more significant in the global perspective was the following statement from findings of the meeting:

We have endeavoured to visualise a position which may exist in the not too distant future, when the Churches on the Mission Field shall have been called to a fuller participation in our common task; and it seems clear to us that the time is drawing near for the formation of national Bible Societies on the same basic principles as our own. Such a development leads us in thought to the vision of a world-federation of Bible Societies, which shall not only facilitate the inter-relations between such national Societies, but shall bear a united witness to the place of the Scriptures in the life of the world and in the growth of God's Kingdom.

The path leading towards a world organisation was thus open. Another step in this direction was the decision, in 1936-7, by the Netherlands Bible Society, the British and Foreign Bible Society and the National Bible Society of Scotland to unify their work in Indonesia. In the summer of 1939 representatives of the American Bible Society, the British and Foreign Bible Society, the Bible Society of France, the National Bible Society of Scotland, the Netherlands Bible Society and the Norwegian Bible Society agreed on the formation of a World Council of Bible Societies. The Second World War prevented its immediate implementation. But in 1946, the bases for the United Bible Societies were laid down at a meeting of Bible Society and Church leaders held in Haywards Heath (England) at the invitation of the American Bible Society and the British and Foreign Bible Society.

This Haywards Heath conference proved to be an historic meeting. This is how J. M. Roe describes it:

The immediate issue to be considered was a very practical one, that of meeting the dire shortage of Scriptures in Europe, but it was recognised that issues of a more strategic nature were bound to be raised. It could scarcely be otherwise in an assembly of such distinction. In addition to officers and committee members of the American, Scottish and Netherlands Bible Societies, there were outstanding Christian leaders from several European countries. They included Bishop Berggrav from Norway, Dr. Hans Lilje from Germany, Archbishop Lehtonen of Finland, Dr. W. A. Visser 't Hooft from Geneva, and many of the European representatives of the B.F.B.S. The two General Secretaries and the Heads of Departments at London Bible House were present, and the opening sessions were presided over by the Chairman of the B.F.B.S. General Committee, Sir Graeme Tyrrell. The Bishop of Chichester, the Right Reverend G. K. A. Bell, a figure well known to the European visitors, also addressed the delegates.

The main, though by no means the exclusive emphasis of the conference was on the spiritual condition and needs of Europe. Of the many matters discussed this was certainly the most critical. There was an insistence on the relevance of the Bible to the re-making of Europe, a continent which more than any other had been subjected to the powerful influence of the printed word. It was recognised that a great co-operative effort was needed, in which the Bible Societies and European Churches must all participate, not only for the circulation, but also for a revival in the use of the Bible. Dr. Temple[7] indicated that this had been a matter of concern to the B.F.B.S. London Committee since early in 1940, and outlined the steps which had been taken even during the years of war to anticipate the need. A voice new in Bible Society circles was then heard. It was that of a young Swiss layman, Monsieur Olivier Béguin, who, in association with Dr. Visser 't Hooft and other leaders of the ecumenical movement in Geneva, had been engaged since 1941 in making what provision was possible for the supply of Scriptures to various parts of Europe, and who described what had been accomplished.

It was generally agreed that a central office for European work was now required, and a number of delegates, including some from the B.F.B.S., favoured Geneva as the place where it should be established. Bishop Berggrav pressed for London to be the centre. The decision was a critical one, because far more than the establishment of a European office was actually involved; what was being established was in fact a prospective world headquarters of the United Bible Societies, of which the eventual character and influence would be determined in no small measure by the place in which it was located.

On the final day of the conference the formation of a body was planned to which the name 'United Bible Societies Council' was given. The concept of a central office for European work was enlarged to that of a headquarters for the new council, provision being made for a branch office in Geneva. Dr. Temple was invited to become secretary of the new body, and his release from administrative duties in the B.F.B.S. was promised in order that he might give the greater part of his time to the new assignment.[8]

[7] Dr. John R. Temple, General Secretary of the British and Foreign Bible Society (1931–46)
[8] J. M. Roe, op. cit., pp. 435–6

So a new world partnership was formed, a partnership which, now that it has come of age, is proving a flexible global instrument in promoting what is clearly a world task. Its objectives were defined thus:

First: to encourage the co-ordination and extension of efforts and develop patterns of effective co-operation among the Bible Societies.

Second: to facilitate the exchange of information among the Bible Societies, in policies as well as in technical problems, and to encourage the harmonisation of policies and techniques.

Third: to supply to Societies such helps and services as can more easily be provided centrally.

Fourth: to collect, assemble and diffuse on a world level and in a global perspective any relevant information and data on world trends, religious developments, and on the various aspects of and progress in the effective use of the Bible in the churches' life and witness.

Fifth: to represent the Bible Societies' movement among the international Christian organisations and further amongst them a better understanding of and greater interest in Scripture distribution as a means of evangelism.

Sixth: to arrange for any emergency service that may be needed on specific occasions.[9]

Since 1946, the work of the United Bible Societies has developed greatly. It is now grouped in four continental regions—Africa, the Americas, Asia—South Pacific, and Europe—each with its coordinating teams for translation, production and distribution. The two main global 'service centres' are in London and New York, and the vast operation is brought together annually in a

[9] For much of the above, I am indebted to a booklet *The United Bible Societies: Brief Historical Notes on the U.B.S. and its Member Societies,* published by the U.B.S. A list of all the member societies and associate members of the U.B.S. may be found as an Appendix to this book (pp. 149–50).

single World Service Budget. It is a good instrument for a great task.

The United Bible Societies was fortunate in its first President (1946–57). Eivind Josef Berggrav was a remarkable man of God.[10] Born in 1884, he early determined to become a pastor and studied theology in Oslo University to that end, taking an active part in the Norwegian Students' Christian Association in which he came under the influence of John R. Mott. He went through a period of severe intellectual doubt and for some years earned his living as a teacher. Slowly his faith returned, now on a firmer basis, and in 1919 he began his pastorate. During these years he wrote a stream of articles and books and in 1929 became Bishop of Hålogaland whence he was translated to Oslo in 1937. He remained Bishop of Oslo until 1951.

It was during these years that he was imprisoned by the Nazis (1942–5). He seemed to have come to the kingdom for such a time as this. At the beginning of the war, he worked hard for peace, interviewing the British Foreign Secretary, Lord Halifax, twice, and Herman Göring once. But peace was not to be, and Berggrav soon incurred the wrath of Quisling. He was suspended from office, and quickly became the recognised leader of the churches in their opposition to Nazism. He was more responsible than anyone else for the document 'The Foundation of the Church', a declaration of faith which was read in the churches on Easter Day 1940 and brought to a head the opposition of Christian men to the threats of the Nazi régime. Berggrav was put under house arrest, and then imprisoned, being kept in solitary confinement. It seems that Quisling wanted to have Berggrav shot, but this plan was frustrated, strangely enough, by the Germans, among whom the Bishop had influential friends including Himmler and von Moltke. A compromise was reached, and Berggrav found himself for three years under house arrest. The conditions of his confinement were very strict, though, with the aid of the disguise given by a small moustache and a pair of glasses, he was able to make a number of

[10] His life has been written under the title *Eivind Berggrav : God's Man of Suspense*, by Alex Johnson, transl. Kjell Jordheim (Augsburg Publishing House, Minneapolis, Minnesota, 1960).

temporary excursions into freedom. He lived a very disciplined life and wrote a great deal. Just before the end of the war, when there was real danger that he might be done away with, he escaped.

Greatly influenced by Archbishop Söderblom of Uppsala and Bishop George Bell of Chichester, Berggrav became a leader in the ecumenical movement. In fact, he was elected one of the presidents of the World Council of Churches. On his death, Dr. Visser 't Hooft said, 'He will be remembered among us as a peace-maker, as a leader of the spiritual Resistance Movement, as a spiritual adviser and friend, as a builder of the World Council of Churches, and *above all as a man of the Bible.*'

The Bible meant much to Berggrav during his internment, as it did also to Martin Niemöller and many others in the long dark years of their captivity. In the closing years of his life, Berggrav gave much time and thought to the work of the Norwegian Bible Society and of the United Bible Societies. On the last day of his life, January 14th, 1959, he drafted a letter to all who were to preach on Bible Mission Sunday the following March. This is how it began:

Bible Sunday? I have the feeling that many of you have paused before this problem—'It is so hard for people to get anything out of Bible reading!' I was bothered by the problem myself for a long time, as if I were shy on behalf of the Bible. Then I received courage to forget my shyness. People *get* something out of reading this 'difficult' book. It was best expressed perhaps by the African woman who said, 'This book *reads* me.' I recommend heartily that people read it.

The next problem? 'There are so many good causes that we have to ask our congregations to consider. Special offerings are not popular.'

This cause, the Bible mission, the Bible for all peoples and tribes—this has priority because it concerns the foundation of all Christianity and because it is right *now* that is important . . .

The letter was never finished. It was found on his desk when he died that afternoon.

Under Berggrav's Presidency, the United Bible Societies had

been established on a sure foundation. The future expansion and development of the work on wise and imaginative lines was guaranteed by the fact that Olivier Béguin continued to be Secretary. Berggrav 'died in faith'—greater things than he could foresee lay ahead. Not least of these was the Biblical vision which was to be given to the Roman Catholic Church at its Vatican Council and the co-operation which was to take place between that Church and the world-wide company of men and women already deeply committed to the cause of Biblical translation and distribution.

The story that led up to this was a long and often bitterly sad one. In 1408, soon after the death of Wycliffe, Archbishop Arundel held a Council at Oxford, and issued the first decree in English Church Law which had to do with Bible reading. The relevant part runs: 'Since it is dangerous, as St. Jerome witnesses, to translate the text of Holy Scripture from one language into another, because in such translations the same meaning is not easily retained in all particulars ... therefore we decree and ordain that no one shall reprint or translate on his own authority any text of Holy Scripture into the English tongue or into any other tongue, by way of book, booklet, or treatise.' The situation was not much better in the next century. A conference of Bishops was held on May 24th, 1530. Following this the King issued a proclamation in the course of which it was said: 'His highness hath therefor ... consulted with the sayd primates ... and by them all it is thought, that it is not necessary, the sayde scripture to be in the englisshe tongue, and in the hands of the common people.' We have seen in an earlier chapter how this restrictive attitude came to be broken down and so 'the word of God was not bound', or, as Moffatt translates it, there was 'no prison for the word of God'.[11] But the odds against this progress were great.

In 1817, Pope Pius VII—with the full concurrence of all the Cardinals—issued a Bull against the Bible Societies in which the design of circulating the Scriptures was characterised as 'an abominable device, by which the very foundations of religion are undermined'; and it was declared to be the duty and the object of the See of Rome 'to employ all means for the purpose of detecting

[11] 2 Tim. 2:9

and rooting out such a pestilence in every way'. The Pope continued: 'For it is evident from experience that the Holy Scriptures, when circulated in the vulgar tongue have, through the temerity of men, produced more harm than benefit.'

Subsequent Encyclicals by Leo IX, Pius VIII, Gregory XVI, and especially Pius IX in 1846 reinforced Rome's stern opposition to what the latter called 'these crafty Bible Societies which renew the ancient guile of heretics and cease not to thrust their Bibles upon all men . . . so that the divine traditions, the teaching of the fathers and the authority of the Catholic Church are rejected'. It cannot be denied, said an early twentieth-century writer, 'that the Bible Societies by invading the Catholic countries and endeavouring to foist the Protestant versions upon a Catholic people, have stirred up much discord, and have laid themselves open to the charge of degrading the Sacred Book by using it as an instrument of proselytism'.

Since the coming of Vatican II a very different attitude has prevailed and a new day has dawned. *The Documents of Vatican II*[12] makes this abundantly clear. The main teaching of the Council on the Bible comes in the *Dogmatic Constitution on Divine Revelation*. This is the most important Council document after the great *Constitution on the Church*. Here it is stated: 'Easy access to sacred Scripture should be provided for all the Christian faithful' (paragraph 22). '. . . all the clergy must hold fast to the sacred Scriptures through diligent sacred reading and careful study . . . They must share the abundant wealth of the divine word with the faithful committed to them, especially in the sacred liturgy . . .' 'Furthermore, editions of the sacred Scriptures, provided with suitable comments, should be prepared also for the use of non-Christians and adapted to their situation. Both pastors of souls and Christians generally, should see to the wise distribution of these in one way or another' (paragraph 25). 'Just as the life of the Church grows through persistent participation in the Eucharistic mystery, so we may hope for a new surge of spiritual vitality from intensified veneration for God's word, which "lasts forever"'

[12] General Editor Walter M. Abbott, S.J. (Guild Press, New York, 1966)

(paragraph 26). Similar emphasis is to be found in other parts of *The Documents of Vatican II*. Thus, for example: 'Sacred Scripture is of paramount importance in the celebration of the liturgy . . . It is necessary to promote that warm and living love for Scripture to which the venerable tradition of both Eastern and Western rites gives testimony.'[13] Again: 'Bible services should be encouraged' (paragraph 35 (4)). There is a footnote to this section which reads: 'Bible services represent both a return to ancient Christian practice and a fuller use of God's Word. A large measure of variety here becomes possible, which will relieve the tedium of repetitious familiar devotions. In line with the scriptural movement, Catholics now have a chance to enrich their spiritual lives by exploring the full treasury of revelation, instead of only a few truths.' And again: 'The treasures of the Bible are to be opened up more lavishly, so that richer fare may be provided for the faithful at the table of God's Word' (paragraph 51).

What a change has taken place! As a step towards implementing the directives of the Council, Pope Paul gave Cardinal Bea, President of the Secretariat for Promoting Christian Unity, a mandate to study Bible needs in the Roman Catholic Church. On April 16th, 1969, Cardinal Bea's successor Monseigneur (now Cardinal) Jan Willebrands, together with Father Walter M. Abbott, S.J., and others were received by the Pope. His address is of such importance that it deserves to be quoted at length:

On April 24th of last year We were pleased to receive the late Cardinal Bea and some of you, who are also present today, at the end of the first conference held in Rome to study how Catholic Biblical Associations and others engaged in the biblical apostolate could implement the very important goals set forth in Chapter Six of the Second Vatican Council's Constitution on Divine Revelation. It is a great consolation to Us that so many others have joined you in this vital work, and that the study has resulted in practical proposals and programmes.

We felt it was a providential thing when Cardinal Bea came to

[13] 'General Principles for the Restoration and Promotion of the Sacred Liturgy', par. 24

Us not long after the close of the Ecumenical Council and asked if the Secretariat which he headed might begin studying the implementation of the final chapter in the conciliar document on the Bible. As a Scripture scholar, Cardinal Bea was esteemed by Christians everywhere; as President of the Secretariat for Promoting Christian Unity, he had won the confidence and even affection of leaders and members of Christian Churches and Communities throughout the world.

We were pleased to approve the Cardinal's request, and We are very grateful that the work for easy access to the Scriptures that he then began has produced such fruitful results: the 'Guiding Principles for Interconfessional Co-operation in Translating the Bible', published on Pentecost Sunday of last year; various programmes of co-operation with the United Bible Societies which have been approved by Episcopal Conferences in many countries and which make the Scriptures available to people who would not otherwise have them; and finally the proposal for an international Catholic Federation for the Biblical Apostolate, which is intended to serve the Bishops in their pastoral responsibilities concerning wider use and knowledge of the Bible.

We understand that this proposal for the International Catholic Federation has been prepared in consultation with the Secretariat for Promoting Christian Unity and representatives of Sacred Congregations concerned with the various aspects of the biblical apostolate. We trust that the details of the plans will be carefully studied and, after approval by the appropriate authority, will be of service to the Bishops throughout the world.

In the course of each day there are many things to which We must give Our attention for the good of the Church and for the good of souls everywhere, but an occasion like this meeting with you today gives Us the welcome opportunity to stress the fundamental importance of God's revealed word in all that We do and say. 'The word of God should be available at all times,' declared the Second Vatican Council. Yes, always, and easily, and ever more widely. It is not only priests, religious brothers and sisters who should have the Scriptures, read them, meditate on them, and meet Christ our Lord daily in this way. As the Second Vatican Council said, 'all the faithful' should have easy access to the Scriptures, in the liturgy, through the Scripture readings and the homily, and also in daily private life. All are called to this meeting with Christ our Lord.

The Second Vatican Council has made it clearer than ever before that We and Our brother Bishops throughout the world have a serious responsibility to do all we can to help provide people with easy access to the Scriptures. When dedicated people like yourselves come forward to help Us in this great task, We rejoice and give heartfelt thanks.

It is a special cause of joy to Us that, as has been said already by Bishop Willebrands, President of the Secretariat for Promoting Christian Unity, co-operation in translating the Scriptures and making them easily accessible to all people results in bringing Christians closer together. If, as has also been said, fraternal collaboration in this work renders the Christian message more credible and appealing to non-Christians, it is clear how much this work should be esteemed by everyone.

For all these reasons, We gladly impart Our special paternal Apostolic Blessing to you, your families and religious communities, your collaborators and supporters.

It had become abundantly clear that close co-operation between Roman Catholics and those who were already engaged in the work of Bible translation and dissemination was called for—and was possible. It was perhaps only natural that, in certain areas such as Latin America, there should be elements of suspicion and recollection of past hurt and even persecution. Occasionally the underground fires still break out into flame. But the change on the part of Rome has been so great, the need of the world is so immense, and the discussions between Roman and non-Roman scholars and administrators are so frank and deep, that leaders in the Biblical movement are convinced that to continue to work separately and to refuse the invitation to collaborate which Vatican II has extended would not only be foolish but would also be sinful. After the meeting of the United Bible Societies Council held at Buck Hill Falls,

Pa., on May 16th–21st, 1966, a statement was issued which included these words: 'We welcome the emphasis of the Second Vatican Council on easy access to the Scriptures for all, and the possibility of co-operation in translation and distribution of the Scriptures generally.' Since then great progress has been made. Who can tell what the effect will be in the renewal of the churches concerned and in the evangelisation of those who hitherto have been unreached by the message of the Bible?[14]

[14] The principles on which co-operation is being worked out can be seen e.g. in: *Guiding Principles for Inter-confessional Co-operation in Translating the Bible*, published jointly by the U.B.S. and the Secretariat for Promoting Christian Unity, June 1968; 'Easy Access to Sacred Scripture for All' by Walter M. Abbott, in *Catholic Biblical Quarterly*, January 1968; and in *Roman Catholics and the Bible*, published jointly by the U.B.S. and the Vatican Department of Common Bible Work, December 1968, revised 1970

7

With Note and Comment

As time goes by, the gap which yawns between the world in which the Bible was written and the world in which we live grows ever wider. It is not simply a matter of the passage of time. The difference is deeper and more subtle than can be measured in terms of centuries. For example, the world in which the Bible was born was a non-scientific world—we do not go to the Bible for lessons in the origin of the universe or in the evolution of the human race. But our world is one which is dominated by technology and which thinks in scientific terms. Nor is this method of thinking confined to the so-called West; as education spreads, as schools and universities multiply throughout the world, these are the thought-forms which increasingly obtain throughout our 'global village'.

Further, the Bible is essentially a rural book. True, St. Paul seems to have confined his missionary activities almost exclusively to the main centres of population and to have been more at home with city metaphors than with country ones. But the fact remains that the desert—that birthplace of prophetic souls—and the country and the small village formed the predominant background against which the Biblical writings were set. Jesus himself was a country man, and his metaphors, parables, and aphorisms make his country and village origins abundantly clear. But today's world is becoming more and more the world of the town and of the big city. The industrial revolution in England has not only involved the drift of millions to great cities (would Plato have dignified them with the description of *polis*?), but it has meant that very few in England are far from the influence of such conurbations. Increasing millions think in urban terms. And what is true of England and of 'the West' generally is becoming increasingly true in Africa and Asia. Urbanisation is reaching out its greedy fingers and bringing under its spell ever increasing numbers of those who only yesterday thought in rural terms. At the same time the effects of technology are, for better *and* for worse, penetrating ever more powerfully into the remaining rural areas.

Again, the Bible is a book whose confines were, roughly speaking, limited to the world of the Near East and of the Mediterranean basin. The centre of events was that little strip of land whose coasts were washed by the eastern extremity of 'the Great Sea' (the Mediterranean). The figures of the Old Testament found themselves involved in the clashes of the great nations which bordered on them—Egypt and Assyria, Babylon and Persia, Greece and Rome. The New Testament figures looked west—to Asia Minor, Rome and Spain. But, broadly speaking, that was their world, and that alone. Today our horizons have been immensely enlarged. There are few corners of the globe, if any, which remain unexplored. 'The world' meant one thing to Amos, even to that intrepid traveller St. Paul; it meant quite another to Wendell Wilkie returning from a world tour during the Second World War and writing 'One World', or even to the schoolboy with his world map open before him.

The world of 'gods many and lords many', as St. Paul half-scornfully described the world of his day,[1] is far removed from that of twentieth-century scientific man. Let the emerging nations continue for a while longer to think in such terms if they will. But for him there is either no god at all (has he not 'come of age', and is he not able to dispense with such childish ideas?), or there is one God, the God, it may be, whose prophet is Mohammed, or the God and Father of our Lord Jesus Christ. But the world of sacrifices, of the shedding of blood, of propitiation of the deity, of temple cult and priestly rite, of defilement and purification, of circumcision and sabbath—this world is to him utterly remote, utterly incomprehensible. It is not that he has grown out of it. He never had any idea of what it was all about.

All this and a great deal more must be borne in mind when, towards the end of the twentieth century, we seek to accomplish the still essential task of putting the Bible into the hands of the

[1] 1 Cor. 8:5

peoples of the world. It is a far more difficult and complex operation than it was when, at the very beginning of the nineteenth century, it was essayed by the founders of the British and Foreign Bible Society. Helps are needed. I would go further and say: helps are essential. Herein lies the wisdom of those who ventured to make the change in the wording of the Charter of the British and Foreign Bible Society to which reference must now be made.

As we have seen, the British and Foreign Bible Society came into being in 1804. In May 1811 its Rule was altered so as to state that the 'sole object' of the Society 'shall be to encourage a wider circulation of the Holy Scriptures *without note or comment*'. That was an admirably clear definition of its task, and it remained unaltered till 1968. In that year, a change was made, and the words 'without note or comment' were omitted. The omission is important. Behind the words 'without note or comment' lies the political controversy of the sixteenth and seventeenth centuries and the sectarian strife of the eighteenth century; the phrase sought to avoid controversy in doctrinal and dogmatic matters. It became clear, however, that, particularly in translations, some measure of explanation (not interpretation) became necessary by means of notes.

In January 1939, after consideration by a sub-committee, the General Committee of the British and Foreign Bible Society passed a carefully worded resolution by which 'note or comment' was defined as interpretative or doctrinal note and comment, and the Rules for Translators enumerated eight types of helps, none of which is generally considered controversial.

At this point the Second World War interrupted normal working and it was not until 1956 and 1960 that the Society was again reviewing its policy of 'note or comment'. In 1960 a meeting of the United Bible Societies Council raised the question of annotated Bibles. In January and May 1961 the British and Foreign Bible Society held meetings with representatives of Churches and Missionary Societies as it was felt that only if they had a clear-cut request from these bodies should they go ahead. Both these meetings failed in their purpose. In 1964 there took place at Driebergen in Holland a conference between officials of the Bible Societies and

Church leaders from all six continents under the chairmanship of the Archbishop of York. Amongst their several recommendations this conference specifically mentioned the desirability of freedom for the Bible Societies to circulate the Apocrypha, and the publication of editions which would include aids for readers as the Churches might agree were necessary.

In 1965 the British and Foreign Bible Society sought from the Privy Council and obtained the amendment of By-law 24 (now re-numbered 23) of its Charter permitting circulation of the Apocrypha upon specific request and with the approval of the General Committee in each case. Still there was 'note or comment', or 'aids to readers' to be dealt with, but the Driebergen Conference had greatly helped to clarify the wishes of the Churches. Driebergen, however, was not alone; pressure for change was coming from many parts of the field.

In April 1967 the British and Foreign Bible Society held another meeting with leaders of the Churches and Missionary Societies. This was completely successful, and, in a unanimous resolution, the meeting welcomed the proposal to provide certain aids for readers and the exploration of prefaces and introductions. With this clear indication of the wishes of the Churches and Missionary Societies the Society was able to have a Special Meeting and, as a result of its decision to seek from the Privy Council the necessary amendments to their Charter and By-laws, in December 1968 the words 'without note or comment' were removed from clause 4(a) of the Charter, and By-law 22 included the proviso that publication and circulation should normally be without 'note or comment' *other than such aids for readers* as should have previously been approved by the General Committee of the Society.

A complete change in the climate of sectarian opinion and feeling in England in the 1960s permitted the British and Foriegn Bible Society to introduce these big emendations to their Charter and By-laws at the urging of the Churches and Missionary Societies and with little opposition.[2]

The omission of the words 'without note or comment' surely

---

[2] I owe the details of the above paragraphs to the kindness of my friend, Brigadier Charles Swift

shows the wisdom of those who were responsible for making it. The one essential object of the Society remains precisely what it has been since its inception—and it is the one essential object of all those other societies which are united under the banner of the United Bible Societies. They are all dedicated to the task of seeing to it that the Bible (in whole if possible, in part if not) is made available in as accurate a translation as can be achieved, in an ever increasing number of languages and dialects, in attractive format, at prices within the reach of those for whom it is intended. It is a highly specialised task, calling for scholarship of the most exact kind, and for skill in printing, binding, packing, shipping, selling, and so on, which make increasing demands on all those concerned. The budget of the United Bible Societies stands at around seven million dollars per annum. This is big business. But without this work, this combination of scholarship and business efficiency, the Church would find itself deprived of the equipment with which from the beginning of its history it has done its work. It would be a crippled Church. So the work must go on, so long as the Church is a missionary Church, that is to say, so long as it seeks to be true to the commission of its Master.

A clear distinction must be made. It is not the task of the Bible Societies to engage in detailed exposition of the Scriptures. That is the abiding work of the churches into whose hands the Bible Societies put those Scriptures. Of this we shall see more later. But there are certain aids without which the Bible may make very little sense once it is in the hands of the readers for whom it is intended. I refer not merely to such things as explanations or illustrations of the flora and fauna of biblical lands, though these are important. A reader who has never been outside the Arctic circle would find it difficult to appreciate 'the lilies of the field'—and anyway they were not what an Englishman means by lilies but something more like scabious.[3] The interpreter who was translating the preacher's text 'I am the good shepherd' in a land where sheep did not exist could hardly be blamed for his version which ran: 'He says he's a good

[3] A. E. Harvey suggests the anthemis or Easter daisy (*The New English Bible Companion to the New Testament*, Oxford University Press and Cambridge University Press, 1970), p. 39

man and keeps goats.' I refer to such aids as glossaries of technical terms which, in some versions, are making an immensely valuable addition to a new translation. A case in point is the glossary at the end of *Today's English Version*, where such words as *covenant*, *defile*, *passover*, *Sadducee* are each given a few words of simple explanation. Again, one thinks of headings, by means of which a long and perhaps complicated passage is broken up and its message made all the clearer by that means. The *New English Bible* has done this on a limited scale. J. B. Phillips in his *Four Prophets* has done it much more liberally.[4]

Art should increasingly be pressed into the service of those who give 'aids' to the understanding of the Bible. In *The Bible for Today*[5] Rowland Hilder and other artists showed what could be done by illustrating the truths of the Bible by a series of black and white pictures in the body of the text, most of them portraying life in the twentieth century. A more recent and outstanding example of the value of such a use of art is to be found in Mlle. Annie Vallotton's work. The daughter of a Swiss writer, she studied art in Strasbourg and now lives in Paris where she often appears on television programmes. She has evolved a method of illustrating the New Testament which, by its very simplicity, somehow brings out the essence of that which she is seeking to depict. She has been impressed with the 'utter simplicity' of Christ's teaching—which is not to deny its profundity—especially the simplicity of his parables. This she has captured. The human figures are universal in application—they might be African, Asian, American, English; there are no facial characteristics. The illustrations are designed to emphasise the point of the story or aphorism—to suggest, to elicit further inquiry, to interest in such a way that the reader identifies himself 'with the biblical characters in their rages, in their hypocrisies, and then perhaps he may learn to smile at himself. And, once we can do this, an important battle has been won.' The words are those of Annie Vallotton herself. There can be little doubt that her illustrations have had much to do with the fact (which we have already noticed)

[4] Published by Geoffrey Bles, 1963
[5] Edited by John Stirling, and published by the Oxford University Press, 1941

that four years after the appearance of *Today's English Version,* some twenty-five million copies have been published.

That there are difficulties connected with the production of 'aids' is not to be denied. The Bible Societies are at the service of all the churches and denominations, and this includes all shades of theological approach. Some churches are fundamentalist and conservative in their approach to the Bible; some are liberal. Some are Anglican, some are Protestant, some are Roman Catholic. The Bible Societies help them all. But this variety of approach means that theological agreement is not always easy. Nevertheless it should be possible, especially in this age of ecumenical understanding, increasingly to agree on such aids as simple 'introductions' to the books of the Bible which would help the newcomer to those books to see what they are about. Such introductions would not usurp the expository function of the Church, but they would decrease the waste entailed by the fact that many readers take up the Bible hopefully, only to cast it aside because they have no key as to its purpose and meaning.

The task of producing aids becomes the more urgent as the distance of our world from that of the Bible increases. The further we move, in time, in thought-forms, in civilisation and culture, from the world in which the Bible came into being, the more imperative does it become to produce, in the very book in which the translation appears, elucidatory matter. This is not to deny for one moment what is undoubtedly a fact, that frequently the Holy Spirit has used passages of Scripture, 'without note or comment', very often in an inaccurate or inadequate translation, to speak to the heart of the reader. His life has been changed, sometimes without any human agency at the start. It is simply to assert that, as any intelligent Christian is in duty bound to bring what grey matter he has to the understanding of the faith, so those who handle the translation and production of the Bible are also under an obligation to produce it in such a form and with such aids as will make it that much easier for the reader to understand.

In view of the gap which yawns between the biblical world and that of the late twentieth century, it would seem obvious that, in the coming years, special care and attention will have to be given to the production and dissemination of particularly significant portions, and selections, of the Bible, rather than of whole Bibles. This becomes all the clearer when factors of population explosion and literacy explosion (which will be considered in the next chapter) are taken into consideration.[6] But factors deeper than those of arithmetic or of financial economy lie behind this argument. Let us suppose that an African or an Asian undergraduate comes into contact with the Bible for the first time. As with any other book he begins at the beginning and very soon finds himself in a world of thought almost wholly unintelligible to him. From one point of view, this is almost more true in the case of an English or American youngster who has been brought up, as so many have, with virtually no education in the Bible, in Christian faith, or in Christian worship. It is likely that he will be attracted to further inquiry and study if his first contact with the Bible is through a book of the New Testament, or through a chapter which deals with some fundamental theme. It will be better still, if that portion is simply and attractively illustrated, perhaps with line drawings (such as those of Annie Vallotton) or with modern photos (such as those with which the American Bible Society has been so boldly experimenting).

It is probable that the Gideons, who have done and are doing good work in supplying Bibles for hotel rooms, schools, and so on, would have met with greater success if, first, they had not shackled the message of the Bible by printing it in a version three and a half centuries old; secondly, if they had used the very substantial aids afforded by modern printing methods; and thirdly, if they had done their work by means of portions and of selections, rather than by providing, at great cost, a complete Bible for every occasion of use.

Let there be no misunderstanding here. We are discussing the initial impact which it is desired to make—the impact of the message of God in Christ on the newly literate man, or on the more sophisticated, better educated man who nevertheless, when he comes into contact with the Bible, finds himself in a totally unfamiliar and perplexing world. We take it for granted that before

[6] *vide infra,* p. 113 ff.

long he must have a complete New Testament in his hands and that eventually, if he is to understand the full sweep of the Biblical revelation, he should be provided with a complete Bible. We are only at pains to make the point that, if misunderstanding and unnecessary perplexity are to be avoided, the first impact is best made by some attractively produced portions, or some carefully made selections, with certain aids attached.

The work of the various Bible reading organisations introduces us to another sphere of work of great importance—the next stage, as it were, in the grand programme which is initiated by the Bible Societies.

The *Bible Reading Fellowship* had its origins in some parish Bible studies undertaken by the Reverend Leslie G. Mannering when he was Vicar of St. Matthew's, Brixton, in South London.[7] He was concerned about deepening the spiritual life of the people in his church. In his parish magazine for December 1921 he warned them of the danger of becoming 'entangled in our own machinery. It is the dynamic of personal religion that really moves men and things. We need to go back to the fundamentals of our faith.' Mannering and his staff looked again at prayer, Bible reading, and Holy Communion, and the place these essentials were occupying in the lives of the Christians at St. Matthew's, Brixton. In regard to the second of these three, they felt the need of a set of readings with brief explanatory notes. In January 1922, 'The Fellowship of St. Matthew' was inaugurated and the first of the monthly leaflets was produced. Within a month, one hundred people had signed on. Soon the number was trebled. Other parishes in other dioceses began to take the notes, and by the time Mannering left Brixton to go to another parish in 1926, the circulation had reached 1,500. Soon the work of helping individuals and groups to an increased knowledge of God through intelligent and devotional reading of the Bible had begun to take on a world-wide aspect.

In origin, the Bible Reading Fellowship was an Anglican movement, and still is predominantly so. But very quickly, the daily

[7] For details, see Margery Sykes, *The Bible Reading Fellowship Story* (Lutterworth, 1958).

Bible readings came to be known in all sections of the Church, and readers were soon to be found scattered through many churches and congregations. It is true to say that the Fellowship has always had an ecumenical content and character. It has not hesitated to call on non-Anglican writers from time to time, and in recent years has invited a Methodist minister, a Congregational minister and a Roman Catholic theologian to sit on its Council. Its most recent venture is the publication of a series of booklets 'Word for the World'. They consist of daily readings, written by churchmen and theologians representing a comprehensive cross-section of the Churches, and including a sequence of historical flashes, beginning with the World Conference of Christian Youth at Amsterdam, 1939, and going on to the Uppsala Conference of 1968.

The address of the Bible Reading Fellowship is 148 Buckingham Palace Road, London, S.W.1 and its Director the Reverend Ian Thomson.

The *Scripture Union* began in 1879 as a branch of the Children's Special Service Mission. More conservative in its approach to the Bible than the Bible Reading Fellowship, it, too, does its work on a world-wide scale and is interdenominational in its outreach. Recently it has been experimenting imaginatively with new methods of approach to readers of all ages. Its address is 5 Wigmore Street, London, W.1 and its General Director Nigel Sylvester.

The International Bible Reading Association arose out of a decision of a committee of the Sunday School Union to find ways of strengthening 'the spiritual work of Sunday School teaching'. A member of that group was Charles Waters, who belonged to the congregation of Charles Haddon Spurgeon. He proposed that an organisation be formed to promote the regular use of the Home Readings scheme which had been launched in 1874. When Waters died in 1910, the I.B.R.A. English-speaking membership had almost reached a million. Since then, the work has progressed, and not only at home. The Association takes very seriously the 'International' part of its title, and produces notes specially designed for use in Africa, Asia and elsewhere. Its address is Robert Denholm House, Nutfield, Redhill, Surrey.

The Soldier's Armoury is, as the title suggests, a Bible reading plan put out by the Salvation Army, but used widely in Anglican and Free Church circles as well as within the Salvation Army. The booklets are more substantial in size than those of the Bible Reading Fellowship and the Scripture Union, but they appear only twice yearly. The address of the Salvation Army is 101 Queen Victoria Street, London, E.C.4.

Response had its origin in the United States of America and is read widely particularly in the Anglican Communion whose cycle of prayer it follows. Each day there is a passage of Scripture, a comment, and then some details about the diocese for which prayer is asked; then a prayer. It is published by Forward Movement Publications and its agent in the United Kingdom is S.P.C.K., 69 Great Peter Street, London, S.W.1.

These and other Bible reading schemes serve to help hundreds of thousands of Christians and inquirers to take an intelligent interest in the actual content of the Bible, to ponder daily on some portion of it, using all the intelligence they have, and to apply to daily living the lessons to be gained from a prayerful reading of Scripture. Often it is found that individual study done in this way leads on to group study. Often those whose appetites have been whetted by these methods are led to deeper and more serious study with the aid of substantial commentaries. Doors are opened into deeper understanding and holier living.

8

The Task Today and Tomorrow

So far we have been concerned with the Bible; with its translation and dissemination; with immediate aids to its understanding through note, comment and illustration within the Bible; with Bible reading notes, and so on. This chapter looks out beyond the field of the Bible and brief aids to its understanding, to the wider field of literature which, while deriving its insights from the biblical revelation, reaches out to men in all facets of their life in a complicated technological society.

The great missionary awakening of the Church which took place roughly at the beginning of the nineteenth century and continued and increased in the following decades (see the beginning of chapter 6) resulted in the establishment of a vast network of Christian institutions. Often these were of the simplest kind imaginable—three walls and a tin- or thatched-roof constituting a village school in India or Africa, or something equally elementary serving as a medical centre in town or country. Often something much more sophisticated and elaborate was created—a church, a cathedral, a hospital, a school or college and, later, a university. The result of this missionary vision and of the obedience of great numbers of men and women in dedicating their lives to its fulfilment was to be seen in bricks and mortar, in the creation of institutions evangelistic, educational and medical, in organisations sometimes conceived in altogether too Western a style but nevertheless bringing the light of the Christian faith and the compassion of the Christian gospel to millions who previously had not come under its spell. Mistakes were made. Of course they were. They were the price paid for obedience to the call to venture. But the influence of wellnigh two centuries of such work has been immense. Again and again, the leaders of the younger nations today are men and women whose early education and whose basic influences have been due to institutions such as those to which we have just referred. Often these leaders have continued as committed Christian men—one thinks of people like Dr. Busia in Ghana. Sometimes they have sat loose to Christian discipleship but the influence of their Christian education has continued and has affected for good their political and sociological policies.

Many of the institutions founded by the Church have now been taken over, wholly or in part, by the governments of the nations concerned. They have money and man-power which, in the nature of the case, are not at the disposal of the Church. In some such institutions it is now forbidden to teach the Christian faith or in any way to seek to make Christian disciples. In others, a happy degree of co-operation between 'Church and State' has been established.

What of the future? No doubt it will be the duty of the Christian Church to found new institutions and to continue to finance and to man old ones. This is likely to be the case especially in areas where governments are less sociologically and philanthropically alert than others. The Church will still have to recruit and train men and women, particularly those with specialist gifts and highly-developed skills, and to provide the necessary finance for the prosecution of their work. But it is wholly likely that the main resources of the Church, in man-power and in finance, in the remaining decades of this century, will need to be concentrated, not on bricks and mortar, not on the founding of new institutions, but on influencing the thinking of men and women by means of the written word and the mass media of radio and television. Christian educationists in universities and schools and Christian doctors must, of course, continue their work of bringing light and health to the peoples of the world. But if the men of influence are to be reached, and if the man in the street is to be reached, with the message of the love of God in Christ, then the mass media must be seen for what in fact they are—superb means to that end. Television, radio, drama, newspapers, magazines, books at all levels, from those designed for the university specialist down to the strip-cartoon designed for the semi-literate—these are the areas of human interest which must be captured.

The task is immense, and can only be faced by long-term strategical thinking and planning. The leaders of the churches must catch the vision of a thorough process of infiltration of the mass media, and of the training of skilled personnel for this task. Sometimes those who undertake this work will be highly-trained experts from the West, supported by the sending churches. Sometimes they will be 'non-professional missionaries', that is to say, men and women who earn their living in posts paid by the local governments or firms or other organisations, but who use every opportunity that presents itself to bear their witness to the Lord whom they serve. This witness may manifest itself in the excellence of the work which they do in the course of their ordinary vocation. It must do this, or else any other witness is stultified. It may manifest itself in the activities in which they engage in out-of-work hours—they may be able to write in the local paper, or speak on the local radio, or appear on some programme—not by any means necessarily always a religious programme—on their local television station. They may be able to lend a hand in the training of native Christians in good writing or in the use of the media of which we are now thinking, for more and more the main burden of this 'infiltration' must fall on the shoulders of the local Christians whose understanding of the native idiom and thought-form will necessarily be closer to the minds of their fellows than that of a 'foreigner' can ever be.

The evidence that is available would seem to suggest that all too little thought has as yet been given by the Church to what we might call the theology and practice of the process of infiltration. It is to be hoped that in the World Council of Churches, in its constituent member churches, in diocesan and local synods, and in parochial church councils (I use the terminology of the Church of England, but I include the parallel bodies in other branches of Christ's Church), this matter will be taken up, debated, prayed over, and acted on. Here is a subject for the great variety of discussion groups which are a feature of Church life in this period of its history—groups whose members, seized of the importance of this matter, could well become the 'ginger groups' of the bigger and more formal organs of church life.

The Task Today and Tomorrow

We have said that the task is immense. It is made all the more formidable for three reasons. *First,* because of the meteoric rise in world population. *Secondly,* because of the high percentage of world illiteracy. *Thirdly,* because of other competitors in the field. Something must be said about all of these.

First, the population explosion. The simplest way to put this is to state that, speaking roughly, it seems certain that the world population will *double* by the end of this century. This calculation allows for massive (if only meagrely successful) programmes of birth control. The brothers William and Paul Paddock, one of whom is an agronomist and the other of whom has spent long years in the United States Foreign Service in undeveloped countries, have written a book *Famine—1975!,*[1] in which they protest against the folly of shutting our eyes to the threat to civilisation which is contained in the fact of population explosion. They hold that this trend can neither be halted nor reversed. They accept the Malthusian formula that population increases by geometrical progression (1–2–4–8–16–32) while food production increases only by arithmetical progression (1–2–3–4–5–6).[2] They calculate that in the middle of this decade the Great Famines will begin—the gap between mouths to be fed and food to fill them will be unbridgeable. They hold that it is unlikely that any techniques of food-production will be found which will be able to influence this trend in such a way as to prevent death by starvation coming not, as today, to tens and hundreds of thousands but to tens and hundreds of millions. It will then be up to the affluent nations of the world to decide which peoples most deserve saving from starvation, for the food supplies even of the most richly endowed nations, such as the United States and Canada, will be totally inadequate to meet the needs of the world at large. It is a terrifying picture to contemplate, both for the rural economist and for the ordinary man who cares for the future welfare of his fellow human beings.

It is fair to add that a more optimistic note is struck by Lester R.

---

[1] William and Paul Paddock, *Famine—1975!* (Weidenfeld and Nicolson, 1969)

[2] Thomas Malthus stated this as long ago as 1798 in his *Essay on the Principle of Population.* It is only recently that people have woken up to take his forecast seriously.

Brown.[3] His theme is that the new 'miracle' rice and wheat seeds are proving to be engines of change on a vast scale and that dramatic successes in raising food output in the poor countries are beginning to dispel the gloomy forecasts of widespread famine and worsening hunger. For the first time in history, it is realistic to consider the eradication of hunger for the overwhelming majority of mankind. A lively appreciation of the work of such men as the Norwegian–American Dr. Norman E. Borlaug (Nobel Peace Prize-winner, 1970), in developing new strains of wheat, must go hand in hand with a caution born of a realistic assessment of facts. Indeed, Dr. Borlaug is himself very cautious. When one such wheat strain was introduced into Pakistan, a rumour spread among the peasants that it would make all the women who ate it sterile. 'If only that were true!', said Dr. Borlaug, 'We should really merit the Nobel Peace Prize. The green revolution cannot cure all ills, but it is a step forward. The problem is simply that too many people are coming on the scene too fast.'

Whatever view be taken of the prophecies of the Paddock brothers, the facts are so serious as to demand the most careful attention. The rate of population explosion is due to a variety of factors, for example the sudden decline in the death rate due to the discoveries of science, and the fact that in most countries of Latin America, Africa and Asia, between 40 and 45 per cent of the population is under the age of fifteen. The vast majority of these young people will shortly themselves be parents. The increase in population is most marked where poverty is worst. Thus it has been reckoned that, while it will take 115 years for the population of Europe to double, it will take only 30 years for Africa and 27 years for Latin America; that in Europe there are 19 births per 1,000 people, while in Africa there are 46, and in Latin America 40. To put it another way, of every 100 additional people born between 1965 and 1985, 85 will live in the 'poor' countries.

If figures on a world scale leave us dazed and stunned, let us take two examples of what is going on in the mid-years of the twentieth

[3] L. R. Brown, *Seeds of Change: The Green Revolution and Development in the 1970s* (Pall Mall Press, 1970)

century. In Brazil, the population has shot up, in the last quarter of a century, from about fifty million to over ninety million. The typical mother at a maternity and child welfare clinic in a working-class suburb of Rio de Janeiro lives on black beans eaten twice a day—she may get a little meat on Sunday. Malnutrition results in chronic illness and lack of energy. Yet child-bearing goes on. The clinics ignore family planning. The Pope's encyclical *Humanae Vitae* (issued in August 1968) did nothing to check the population explosion in a predominantly Roman Catholic country, and there is a real danger—so one of Rio's most famous children's doctors has warned—that Brazil will sink to the level of mass human suffering of a 'second India'. (In India, the population rises at the rate of a million a month. Let this be noted. The figure is not that of new births. It allows for deaths. Population *increases* by twelve million a year.)

Our second example comes from Jamaica, a small island not rich in natural resources (except bauxite). Its population is roughly one and three-quarter million. That population grows at the rate of one every nine minutes. Where is food to be found for these 50,000 new mouths every year? Where are places in school to be found? Where employment for school-leavers?[4]

Turning again from particular examples to the world scene, it is estimated that by 1986, 35 per cent of the people of the world will be less than fifteen years old. Even today China has more children under the age of ten than the total population of Russia. It does not take a great deal of imagination to envisage those figures in terms of population explosion. No wonder that Sir Julian Huxley has written, 'Over-population is the most serious threat to human happiness and progress in this very critical period in the history of the world.'

Now, our concern in this book is not that of belly-hunger. It is that of hunger of spirit and mind. The figures given in the preceding paragraphs present a picture of a problem at which the mind boggles—but for the Christian a problem is also an

[4] I am indebted to *Probe 1: Population and Family Planning* (Text by Eric Jay. Published by S.C.M. Press in conjunction with the Christian Education Movement, 1969)

opportunity and a challenge, and this problem must be viewed as such.[5]

Secondly, illiteracy. How do we define the term? It has been said that a people cannot be described as truly literate until it enjoys the capacity to produce and to appreciate *literature*. That is true; but when we speak of illiteracy we think of something more elementary than that. To be functionally literate, as distinct, let us say, from being just able to sign one's name or make out single words, one must be able to read, for example, simple instructions, write a letter, keep some kinds of record. If this is literacy, then it appears that something like a *thousand million adults are illiterate*—'adult' being used of anyone aged fifteen or over.

Vast numbers like a thousand million are difficult to envisage, and abstract concepts like illiteracy are hard to grasp. Let us put this matter in concrete terms. I use the words of Sir Charles Jeffries, to whose book *Illiteracy: A World Problem*[6] I am greatly indebted in this section; a book, moreover, which should be compulsory reading for all who wish to grapple with this problem. He writes: ' "The illiterate" is a man, or woman, who is condemned to a status which, in the circumstances of today, is less than human. The illiterate is a man, who, having scraped together ten shillings to meet the tax collector's demand, cheerfully walks away with a receipt showing that he has paid five shillings. The illiterate is a mother who has to trust someone else to read her letters from her absent son and send him her replies. The illiterate is a farmer who cannot decipher the simple instructions which could save his crop from disaster. The illiterate is a woman whose baby is dying of some malady which the poster on the wall tells how to prevent or cure. The illiterate is a man who goes on a train journey not knowing whether he has been charged the proper fare, not able to read the

[5] The problem of population explosion is put succinctly and clearly in a chapter entitled 'Too Many People?' in *Man in his Living Environment: an Ethical Assessment* (A Report by the Board for Social Responsibility, Church Assembly, 1970). This valuable 80-page booklet, brought out in time for use during European Conservation Year 1970, sets the problem in the wide context of ecology, air- and water-pollution, conservation, and so on. See also G. Rattray Taylor, *The Doomsday Book* (Thames and Hudson, 1970), especially chapters 9 and 10

[6] Charles Jeffries, *Illiteracy: A World Problem* (Pall Mall Press, 1967)

destination named on his ticket or the names of the stations through which he passes. The illiterate is an old woman crying because she envies her granddaughter who can go to school, a man who can only count on his fingers, a woman who told her teacher that she must learn to read as she was tired of getting on to the wrong bus.'[7]

That brings it home! A thousand million adults like that! And *this* problem is inextricably linked with the hunger problem; for 'the map of hunger and the map of illiteracy in the world are the same'.[8] To put this another way: tackle the problem of illiteracy in some backward country, and you have made the first substantial inroad on the problem of famine and undernourishment.

If one studies a map made to illustrate world illiteracy, the results are highly interesting—one such is given at the beginning of Sir Charles Jeffries' book. It becomes clear that the illiteracy rate is only slight in most of the countries of Europe, in most of North America and parts of South, in Australia and New Zealand, etc. In large parts of Latin America and elsewhere, it varies from 5 to 50 per cent of the population, while in Africa it is reckoned at 78 to 84 per cent, in the Arab countries at 78 to 82 per cent, and in Asia and Oceania 53 to 57 per cent. (The figures are necessarily rough and are dated 1962, but they are sufficient to give a general idea of the problem.)

The immensity of the problem and the size of the figures must not depress us. There is much evidence to show that when illiteracy is tackled, particularly at government level, it can be radically reduced if not virtually eliminated. Russia, under the leadership of Lenin who viewed illiteracy as 'Enemy Number One', set out to eliminate it in 1920. The census of 1959 recorded a literacy rate of 98·5 per cent. In the Philippines the literacy rate has risen from about 5 to 75 per cent in forty-four years. In countries such as Brazil, Bolivia, and Zambia campaigns are in progress to reduce the curse of illiteracy. One of the most imaginative schemes is that which is now operating in Iran, under the direct leadership of the

[7] ibid., p. 13
[8] ibid., p. 9, quoting from 'Illiteracy Spells Hunger', reprinted from UNESCO *Courier*, February 1963, p. 2

Shahanshah. In an address which he delivered in 1968 at the Commencement Ceremony of Harvard University, he described the world illiteracy situation as 'frightening, both from the moral and human standpoints. Speaking strictly economically, it is leaving unutilised a huge human capital because of the ignorance of vast numbers of people.' He went on to describe an 'extensive experiment which is being carried out in my country . . .' It is called 'The Armies of Iran's White Revolution', which consist of conscripts who perform their national service in the Literacy Corps, the Health Corps, and the Development Corps, and who otherwise would have served in the rank and file. It is the first of these three corps which is of immediate interest to us. Most of the eighteen months of these young men's service are devoted to teaching people to read—the young during the day, the adults at night. Systematically the work goes on, with supervisors responsible for the groups of young men. By January 1970 over 56,000 young men and over 4,000 young women had served in this way, thus making some 1·5 million adults and children literate. Over 50 per cent of these young people have decided to continue as teachers in the villages, building schools and teaching old and young. Thus the illiteracy rate is made to fall steadily. With this successful experiment in his mind, the Shahanshah suggested that, under the aegis of the United Nations, a Universal Welfare Legion should be formed, the members of which would be committed to the task of erasing those curses which prevent men and women from achieving their full humanity.

It is 'sheer, stark, staring lunacy'—to use the words of Sir Charles Jeffries[9]—that the world with all its wealth and resources, should allow the problem of illiteracy to wait for a solution. 'Whether we reach the moon is quite unimportant in comparison to the question whether we will help human beings to live and to live as human beings are meant to live.' So wrote Dr. Visser 't Hooft.[10] Since he wrote, the moon has been reached; but how big a dent has been made in the problem of illiteracy? Governments must be urged to act, and to act magnanimously. UNESCO must

[9] ibid., p. 160
[10] *The Listener*, March 1967

be supported, and especially the Literacy Division of its Department of Adult Education and Youth Activities. The lessons of pioneers like Dr. Frank Laubach must be pressed home. Illiteracy must be seen for the curse that it is, and treated accordingly.[11]

Thirdly, other competitors. As the world population explodes, and as millions of children in the ordinary course of their education and millions of adults as the result of literacy campaigns learn to read, there will be—there already are—many competitors for access to the opening minds of the newly literate masses. The market is wide open.

The Times in its Saturday Review[12] had an article entitled 'A Book to Caress'. The book referred to was the little red book of the quotations of Mao. I quote from the article: 'In the last year or so it (the book) has transformed the Chinese into so many pupils devoted to the ipse dixit. The book is carried round to show that one has it; thus we have demonstration, rather, ostentation of the book. It is waved in the air at meetings, parades, and gatherings; thus we have exaltation of the book, or threat and challenge by means of the book. It is opened and glanced at, and thus we have consultation. It is read aloud in answer to someone, and thus we have citation, communication. Closed, it is caressed with the hand or pressed to the heart, and thus we have affection. It is held in the hand during dances, songs and propaganda recitals, and thus we have symbolisation . . . It is incredible, actually, how much a little book like Mao's can influence man's behaviour.' The thoughts of Mao are proving to be one of the most 'successful' of the competitors for the minds of men in this century. 'A drop of ink makes millions think.' This drop of ink has done just that, and brought untold millions under the domination of the Cultural Revolution. There is a parallel between Mao's little book and the Koran which Mohammed gave to the Arab peoples. Both books have moulded and are moulding the thinking of nations.

Perhaps even more subtle than the *Thoughts of Mao* in its competition for the minds of men is the approach of materialism. This is pitiless in its persistence. The stories in the newspapers, the

[11] See further Appendix II, pp. 150–151
[12] October 26th, 1968

119

advertisements on the hoardings, the themes of the films shout the message that the one thing that matters is material success. To acquire, to grasp, to hold, to possess—these are the verbs that tell; to *be* is comparatively unimportant. A larger car, a better television set, a more expensive mink coat, a more glittering ring—by these success is to be measured. Own these, and you have arrived. Miss out on these, and you have failed. This competition for the minds and affections of men is, of course, particularly powerful in the affluent West, but the infection is spreading like a cancer, and one has only to travel, say, in Africa or India to see how powerful is its spell.

Then, too, there is the competition of pornography. Here a trade on a world scale appears to be operating. It is notoriously difficult to define accurately what is meant by pornography, or to draw a distinct line between the bounds of good literature aimed at truly depicting the contemporary scene and that which is merely designed to titillate and corrupt. Certain recent legal cases have served to illustrate this. Further, many who would otherwise wish to bring a legal action against the writers or publishers of books which they consider indecent are inhibited from doing so because of the unsatisfactory legal definition of pornography.[13] (According to the Obscene Publications Act 1959, an article is deemed to be obscene if its effect if taken as a whole is such as to tend to deprave and corrupt persons who are likely, having regard to all relevant circumstances, to read, see or hear the matter contained or embodied in it.) They realise also that bringing a legal action necessarily draws attention to the particular book concerned and ensures a rapid rise in its sales! (In a very different context, Lord Shaftesbury discovered this, to his chagrin, as long ago as 1866. He referred in a speech to Sir John Seeley's *Ecce Homo* as the 'most pestilential book ever vomited, I think, from the jaws of hell', a phrase which Seeley reckoned sold 10,000 copies and put £1,000 into his pocket![14])

[13] On this thorny subject, see *Obscene Publications: Law and Practice*, issued by the Board for Social Responsibility of the General Synod of the Church of England, 1970
[14] Owen Chadwick, *The Victorian Church*, part II, p. 65

The Task Today and Tomorrow

But, nice distinctions apart, there is no doubt that every year there pours from the presses of the world, and it would seem particularly from the United States of America and latterly from Denmark, a flood of literature which can only serve to poison the minds of men. Every year, the police of this country burn at the docks many tons of such material. According to articles written by a team of investigators into the pornographic bookshops of London and three other large towns,[15] 'at Scotland Yard, the Obscene Publications Squad ... has fourteen men who devote almost all their time to the pursuit and seizure of filth ... They have now a stock of *seventy-five tons* of obscene material ... Even this enormous amount represents only a small proportion of what they seize: they keep a consignment only till a court has ordered the conviction of the former owner, and then they burn it or send it for conversion into pulp.' Thus, under the various legal enactments in England concerned with obscene publications, the following were seized by Customs: In 1966–7 there were 165 trade seizures involving one and a quarter million magazines and 205,000 books; in 1967–8 there were 245 trade seizures involving 612,000 magazines and 324,000 books; in 1968–9 there were 164 trade seizures involving 792,000 magazines and 703,000 books.

Mr. Charles Keating, President Nixon's nominee to the United States Commission on Obscenity and Pornography, speaking to a press conference at the American Embassy in London in the spring of 1970, said that the pornographic industry in America was variously estimated at between five hundred million dollars and two thousand million dollars. An article in the *Scotsman*,[16] referring to the contribution of pornography to the Danish balance of payments, says that, while there are no reliable statistics, that contribution could be in the region of fifty million Kroner (£2·7 million) a year, though the article cautiously adds the words 'according to informed guesswork'.

It is impossible to estimate what is the effect on the minds and morals of the citizens of the world of this vast effluent of pornographic writing. There are those who would tell us that it does not

[15] *The Sunday Telegraph*, May 8th and 15th, 1966
[16] March 19th, 1970

cause sexual offences and does not corrupt youth. President Johnson's Commission on Obscenity and Pornography recently concluded that there is 'no evidence that exposure to or use of explicit sexual materials plays a significant role in the causation of social or individual harms such as crime, delinquency, sexual or non-sexual deviancy or severe emotional disturbances. There is no warrant for continued governmental interference with the full freedom of adults to read, obtain or view whatever such material they wish.' The Commission's report, which was published during President Nixon's term of office, was repudiated by the President himself as 'performing a disservice'. He argued, with some force, that if pornography has no lasting effect on man's character, 'it must also be true that great books, great paintings and great plays have no ennobling effect. Centuries of civilisation and ten minutes of commonsense tell us otherwise.' While stressing the importance of freedom of expression, the President said that 'pornography is to freedom of expression what anarchy is to liberty.'

The Senate followed the President's lead and rejected the Report by sixty votes to five. It looks as if the sex-pedlars have overdone it. Certainly some very searching questions would seem to be called for as to the kind of methodology used in reaching the astonishing conclusions of the Report. Greater weight should be given to the arguments used by Pamela Hansford Johnson in her book *On Iniquity: Some Personal Reflections arising out of the Moors Murder Trial.*[17] Here this well-known writer and novelist breaks a lance with those who too readily assert that there is no such thing as wickedness, there is only sickness. Taking the hideous Moors case as a kind of touchstone, she seeks to examine the things which encourage people in wickedness or which 'break down those proper inhibitions which have hitherto kept the tendency to it under restraint'. She notes that Brady and Myra Hindley, the two main criminals concerned in the case, had a library of some fifty books of a 'sado-masochistic, titillatory and sado-Fascist' kind, nearly all of which could be picked up in bookshops though one or two might have been smuggled in. Miss Hansford Johnson has little doubt in her own mind that there was a connection between the pabulum

[17] Pamela Hansford Johnson, *On Iniquity* (Macmillan, 1967)

on which the criminals fed their minds and the deeds which those same criminals perpetrated. Her courageous book makes the point that the almost total permissiveness of what is allowed to be sold on our bookstalls, generally in paperbacks, is of enormous danger to the public and especially to the young. She is brave enough to face the wrath of those who would malign her for encouraging some degree of censorship, believing as she does that much of what is hailed as 'courageous' is not published because it is good writing but because the stuff has money in it and brings a quick and sure turn-over. 'When the Sermon on the Mount was bundled into the dustbin . . . a moral vacuum was created: and the liberal humanists have not succeeded in filling it.'

Competitors, then, for the minds of men are keen. Rival ideologies, the claims of materialism, the lure of pornography—in mentioning these we have only touched on some of the more obvious. The truth is that these competitors, together with the fact of the meteoric rise in world population, face the Christian Church with perhaps its biggest challenge since the day of its birth.

How is this challenge to be met? Quite clearly it can only be met on a basis of the closest possible ecumenical co-operation. Unity is strength. Whatever denominational tensions may arise must be faced in full realisation of the need of the world and of the strength of the opposition ranged against the Church of Christ. Christians cannot afford to work separately or to waste their resources of manpower, skill, and money. The example of the Bible Societies, which (as we have seen) have worked since the inception of the British and Foreign Bible Society in 1804 on an inter-denominational basis and are now working in co-operation with the Roman Catholic Church, should be their inspiration.

We have already noticed, in passing, the work of the Society for Promoting Christian Knowledge.[18] One of the main purposes of its foundation in 1698 was 'to disperse, both at home and abroad, the Bible and tracts of religion'. To this day it carries on important work in encouraging and publishing in book and pamphlet form literature on theological and other subjects. In its work it has been greatly helped by the Society (now, since its union with the

[18] *vide supra*, p. 83

Universities Mission to Central Africa, the United Society) for
the Propagation of the Gospel in foreign parts (founded in 1701).
These are Anglican foundations. But the Religious Tract Society,
founded in 1799, was, like the British and Foreign Bible Society,
inter-denominational from the start, its management being shared
equally between churchmen and nonconformists. Among its first
supporters were such well-known Evangelicals as Zachary Macaulay, Edward Bickersteth and Legh Richmond. Its first Secretary
was Joseph Hughes, a Baptist minister who was later to be the first
nonconformist Secretary of the British and Foreign Bible Society.
In 1941, the Religious Tract Society became the United Society
for Christian Literature, by an amalgamation of the Religious Tract
Society, the Christian Literature Society for China, and the Religious Tract Society of China. Thus the Religious Tract Society
(U.S.C.L.) and the British and Foreign Bible Society have led the
way, from days long before the kind of ecumenical co-operation
which is now common, in united endeavour in this field of Christian
literature.

That co-operation was needed, both between denominations and
between the many different agencies working to provide Bibles and
Christian literature, became glaringly obvious in the 1960s. If any
kind of worthwhile impact was to be made in this realm on the
rapidly growing population of the world, the Church of Christ just
could not afford to work as it were in segments. The work is highly
technical, beset with problems which can be met only by a combination of the best brains and skills which the churches can provide. The Christian conscience began to be alerted to this. Thus,
for example, in New Delhi in 1961 the need of the world for Bibles
was presented to the third Assembly of the World Council of
Churches. In Tokyo in 1963, the United Bible Societies launched,
under the title 'God's Word for a New Age', a campaign to treble
the world circulation of Scriptures within three years. In
Driebergen in 1964, leaders of the churches from all over the
world met to prosecute plans for further extension of the work. In
Uppsala in 1968, another presentation of the work of the Bible
Societies was made to the fourth Assembly of the World Council
of Churches.

Years before this series of conferences, A. M. Chirgwin, Research Secretary of the United Bible Societies between 1951 and 1956, had reported the result of a three-year study on the place given to the Bible in the evangelistic outreach of the Church. This he did in a booklet entitled *The Bible in World Evangelism*.[19] E. H. Robertson, study secretary of the United Bible Societies, through such studies as *The Recovery of Confidence* (1961), *The Bible in East Germany* (1961), *The Bible in the British Scene* (1961), *Methods of Bible Study* (1962), and *The Bible in the Local Church* (1963),[20] recorded his own studies in readable form for a large public. S. J. de S. Weerasinghe, Asia study secretary of the United Bible Societies, in a series of booklets published[21] in 1964 and 1965, did similar work for a predominantly Asian public. G. H. Wolfensberger, the most recent of the study secretaries, has, in his books *Multiplying the Loaves*[22] and *The Indispensable Old Testament*,[23] challenged Christians and churches to ask themselves what they should be doing to provide the Scriptures in meaningful language for all who can read.

So the essential nature of the work of the Bible Societies came to be increasingly acknowledged and supported by the large number of churches which made up the membership of the World Council as well as by others who owed no allegiance to that Council. Indeed, incidentally, that common interest has done something to bridge the gap which yawns between these two great bodies of Christians.

In addition to the actual work of providing Bibles, Testaments and portions, much was being done, as we have seen, to provide also Christian literature of a wider kind. There were, however, two great drawbacks in the prosecution of this work. First, there was all too little co-operation between the agencies devoted to this task. This impeded progress and entailed waste. Secondly, the work

[19] A. M. Chirgwin, *The Bible in World Evangelism* (S.C.M., 1954, Wyvern Books, 1961)
[20] All published by the S.C.M. Press
[21] All published for the U.B.S. by the Christian Literature Society
[22] G. H. Wolfensberger, *Multiplying the Loaves* (Fontana, 1968)
[23] G. H. Wolfensberger, *The Indispensable Old Testament* (Netherlands Bible Society, for U.B.S.)

held a place far too low on the list of priorities of the great majority of Christian people at least in this country.

It was considerations such as these which led to the launching in 1964 of a movement to 'Feed the Minds of Millions'. Its object was two-fold—to increase the revenues of the British and Foreign Bible Society and the National Bible Society of Scotland, and to raise a large sum for Christian literature especially in the newly-developing nations. The Bible Society was anxious to take its share responsibly in meeting the challenge issued by the United Bible Societies in Tokyo in 1963 to treble the world circulation of Scriptures within three years. The World Council of Churches had initiated a Christian Literature Fund, of which Britain's share was £100,000. The Feed the Minds campaign undertook the responsibility of raising this sum—and kept its promise.

The campaign was launched at St. James' Palace, London, in the presence of Her Majesty The Queen Mother, the Archbishops of Canterbury and York, the Prime Minister (Mr. Harold Wilson), heads of the major denominations, and civic leaders from all over the country. For the first three years, the money raised was shared between the Bible Society and the cause of general Christian literature. After three years, the Bible Society, though still deeply interested in the campaign, became responsible for its own appeal and promotion. So from January 1968 Feed the Minds continued its increasing work through Joint Action for Christian Literature Overseas. This meant joint planning of literature and joint planning of appeal for money and spending of money. Joint Action for Christian Literature Overseas was sponsored by the Society for the Promotion of Christian Knowledge, the United Society for Christian Literature, and the Christian Literature Council of the Conference of British Missionary Societies.

Thus closer planning and co-operation was achieved than had ever been the case before. Wastage was greatly reduced. World needs were jointly considered. It is much to be hoped that soon the day will arrive when 'Feed the Minds' will be a slogan as well known as 'Oxfam', for the work of the former is at least as urgent as—many would say even more urgent than—the work of the latter.

The Task Today and Tomorrow

The policy of Feed the Minds was early formulated as follows:

To extend to all men the insights of the Christian Gospel, in its bearing on their personal, social and national relationships. A fundamental part of this work is the provision of truly educational material which will help people of all races and creeds, especially the newly literate, to free themselves from ignorance, hunger and disease.

Work is now going on which could not have been done had it not been for a growing stream of grants made from Feed the Minds funds—work in Iran and Uganda, in India and Latin America, in fact all over the world. The underwriting of Christian newspapers such as *New Day* in Uganda, the setting up of a new bookshop in Brazil, the sending out of light mobile units with audio-visual equipment and Land-Rovers for tougher work in literature evangelism, the launching of new ventures in book production and distribution, and the establishing and strengthening of centres in which nationals can be trained in writing, broadcasting, printing and so on—these and many other ventures have been made possible or have been under-girded by grants from Feed the Minds. It is increasingly being realised that it is almost impossible for a Westerner to write effectively for, let us say, an African or an Asian reading public. There are very few such who can both master the idiom of people of nations other than their own and can become one with them in their ways of thinking and reacting. It is, therefore, of first importance that our best skills should be put into such ventures as the Literature and Radio Centre at Mukono, where nationals are helped in learning the difficult arts of writing, broadcasting, and distributing literature. Here in England, under its Executive Director, Mr. David W. Lomax, the Christian Communication Centre is helping workers in the field of communication overseas, by giving information and advice on audio-visual materials and equipment, a highly necessary service in an age when the helps of technology should be used to the full in the service of the Christian Gospel. Here again the basis of the work is interdenominational.

The task is immense—not only because of the swiftly increasing numbers of people to be reached (as we have seen) but because of the scope of the literature required. 'Feed the Minds'; when a Christian uses the phrase, what content does he give to the word 'feed'? With what are the minds of men to be fed? There is no doubt that first and foremost comes the Bible, in whole or in part. Then all kinds of literature which can be broadly labelled theological—from strip cartoons for the almost illiterate and the very newly literate to theological books, written in the idiom of the people, for the universities and theological colleges of the developing nations. Under the heading 'theological' may well be included liturgical material for public worship as well as aids to private devotion. Here is an immense field; why should we expect an African or an Asian or a Latin American to pray as we do in twentieth-century England, least of all using the language and thought-forms of the period of the first Elizabeth?

But the Christian is a follower of the *incarnate* Lord. As such, he is committed to the belief that there is no area of human life which should not come under his domination; there is no sphere of human activity which is not of interest to him. Home, work, leisure, politics, drama, art—'the earth is the Lord's and the fulness thereof'. It matters to the Creator God that his gifts are used responsibly by those to whom he has entrusted them; that the air and the lakes and the seas should not be polluted; that the earth should not be turned into a dust-bowl by misuse of the soil; that the decisions of politicians should reflect the mind of the Maker in their effect on his children; that his gift of sex should be used responsibly; that leisure should be spent creatively. If this is so— and what Christian dare question it?—then the minds of Christians, and especially of new Christians, must be fed accordingly, and this kind of mind-feeding must be seen as Christian activity of the first importance.

The field is the world; and the task, we repeat, immense in its scope.

9

'In Full Assurance of Faith'

The phrase, which comes from the Epistle to the Hebrews,[1] refers to that confidence which is the right of a Christian worshipper in his approach to God. In this final chapter we use it, out of its original context, of the confidence which the Christian may have in his mission to the world.

It cannot be said that such confidence is an outstanding mark of the Church in the closing decades of the twentieth century. On the contrary, the witness of the Church has often been marked by hesitancy and loss of nerve. The possibility—even the desirability—of anything in the nature of proclamation has been questioned. Dialogue? Yes. Discussion? Yes. Asseveration—affirmation of 'the things most surely believed among us'? That is a very different matter. Timidity and lack of confidence are the last accusations that can be levelled against the Church of the first century. The same can hardly be said of that of the twentieth.

There are, however, significant reasons why Christians today should move forward to a recovery of confidence—and that not least in the sphere of their understanding and use of the Bible and so of their approach to the world with that Bible and with literature whose insights derive from it.

The period which has seen the greatest activity in human history in the translation and dissemination of the Bible has been also the period of the most searching and intensive criticism of the Bible. This is not something to be regretted but, rather, welcomed. It was Sir Edwyn Hoskyns who said that 'the critical and historical study of the New Testament is . . . the prime activity of the Church'.[2] The reverently critical study of the Bible must constantly engage

[1] Heb. 10:22
[2] Sir Edwyn Hoskyns and Noel Davey, *The Riddle of the New Testament* (Faber and Faber, 1931), p. 10

the minds of those who are concerned with interpreting the message of the Bible to contemporary society. The point has been well made by the Archbishop of Canterbury: 'The hearing of the word in the Bible, and the pursuit of critical study are in no way incompatible. It is necessary to reject the idea that a firm faith implies the repelling from the mind of the queries raised by criticism—for the faith of a Christian is faith in God, and God is the giver of the scholar's quest for truth as he sets out in search of it, as one not knowing whither he goes. It is required of faith that it does not deny the spirit of inquiry; and conversely it is required of the spirit of inquiry that it does not cling to prejudices as to what God can or cannot do in the sovereign activity of his word'.[3]

To this position thus outlined by Dr. Ramsey most Christians would today gladly assent. But the road which has led to this position has been long and uphill. It was not many generations ago that doubt was labelled as sinful to a Christian; and Pusey, so Dr. Owen Chadwick reminds us,[4] recommended men even to 'extirpate curiosity'! A reading of the first three chapters of Dr. Chadwick's second volume of *The Victorian Church*—the chapters entitled 'Science and Religion', 'History and the Bible' and 'Doubt'— shows how uphill that road was, particularly from the 1860s onwards. Much for which men of that period were indicted as heretics or even taken to court is now the commonplace of biblical scholarship. We who enjoy the fruit of their labours must not forget the cost at which that fruit was achieved. Today it is possible to combine scientific biblical criticism with a belief in the Bible as an authoritative word of God; to see in the Bible the record of certain central historical facts, together with symbolic interpretation conveyed through drama, poetry and allegory.[5]

The biblical story is, as the Germans have it, *Heilsgeschichte*, salvation-story. It is precisely this which gives it its relevance to life, and which gives it its unity, so that we can speak of this library

[3] A. M. Ramsey in Peake's *Commentary on the Bible* (Nelson, revised edn. 1962), p. 7
[4] *The Victorian Church*, part II, p. 124
[5] On this, see further the article by Dr. A. M. Ramsey quoted above, and the bibliography appended to that article

of books—thirty-nine of them in the Old Testament and twenty-seven of them in the New—as *the* Bible. Both these points are worth elaborating. Relevance and unity are inter-related.

On the face of it one would scarcely expect to find the Bible relevant, for consider the world from which it comes and contrast the world in which we moderns live. It comes straight out from the ancient world. True, it is not very ancient. *Six Thousand Years of The Bible* is the name of a book by G. S. Wegener. But what is six thousand years in the evolution of man, or in the emergence of our tiny planet in the vast universe of which it is an infinitesimally small part? In that perspective, Abraham was alive last night and Moses was at work this morning. Nevertheless, it is an ancient book, even though we now know that many of the stories and the thought-forms of the people who gave us the Bible were dependent on those of peoples more ancient than themselves. And what an extraordinary mixture the Bible is—a mixture of 'old unhappy far off things, and battles long ago' and love stories, of myth and ritual, of poetry and prose, of letters and theological theses, of history and apocalyptic. Here cries for vengeance—'happy shall he be, that taketh and dasheth thy little ones against the stones'[6]—mix with passages of infinite tenderness—'can a woman forget her sucking child, that she should not have compassion on the son of her womb? Yea, they may forget, yet will I not forget thee.'[7] Here great passages of mighty doctrine, which have affected the history of human thought and indeed of national government, mix with intimate requests from a man in prison for a cloak and for 'all my note-books',[8] or for a room ready for him when he arrives.[9] Here parables of Jesus—who 'spoke of lilies, vines and corn, the sparrow and the raven'—jostle dark and threatening outpourings of apocalyptic vision, in which distress of nations is depicted under the imagery of natural and supernatural upheavals. Here the contributions of the nations converge—the rivers of Hebrew, Egyptian, Babylonian, Persian, Greek thinking flow together. Who can read

[6] Ps. 137:9
[7] Isa. 49:15
[8] 2 Tim. 4:13
[9] Philem. 22

Proverbs—still more Ecclesiasticus—without seeing a confluence of Greek and Hebrew minds, each enriched by the other? Here is an extraordinary amalgam. In face of this, ought one to speak of the Bible in the singular at all? True, we get the word 'Bible' from the Latin *biblia* which is a feminine singular, but that feminine singular is the Latinising of a Greek neuter plural—*ta biblia*. Were the Romans right in making a singular out of a plural? Or, to put the question more theologically and less philologically, is there a unity within these sixty-six books which justifies us in speaking of 'the Bible', an overmastering theme which allows us to speak of this conglomeration of writings in the singular? Is this strange library of books, this collection which reflects the interaction of so many nations down so many centuries, simply a collection of ancient writings, to be put on our bookshelves with the Vedas and the Upanishads or alongside of Plato and Ovid? Or can it also be called a modern book because of its relevance to modern man in his living, his thinking, his conduct of himself and of his affairs? Is there a master-theme which ties the sixty-six books together and makes the contributions of the nations captive to it? Has it a word of eternal significance to man, whether that man be the sophisticated creature of a highly developed scientific culture or whether he belongs to a pattern of society which has as yet hardly felt the impact of Western civilisation?

One can here do little more than indicate three areas in which the relevance of the Bible to modern man can be seen, three themes which tie its books together into a unity—man, God, and life.

(i) *Man.* The down to earth realism of the Bible on this subject is impressive. Shakespeare makes Hamlet say, 'What a piece of work is a man! How noble in reason! how infinite in faculty! in form and moving how express and admirable! in action how like an angel! in apprehension how like a god! the beauty of the world! the paragon of animals!'[10] There is that in the Bible to which Shakespeare might have appealed for corroboration when he wrote this. In one of the creation stories of Genesis, when God had made man, with his procreative powers and his authority over

[10] *Hamlet* II. ii. 315–20

nature, he saw what he had made 'and behold, it was very good'.[11]
The Psalmist, even with his tiny view of what constitutes the
universe, sees how small is man in comparison. 'Yet,' he goes on,[12]
'thou hast made him little less than God, and dost crown him
with glory and honour. Thou hast given him dominion over the
works of thy hands; thou hast put all things under his feet.' He
elaborates 'all things' in terms of man's mastery over cattle, birds
and fish. Had the Psalmist been living in the twentieth century A.D
instead of several centuries B.C. he would no doubt have spoken of
man's mastery over bacteria and the problems of space flight and
so forth.

'What a piece of work is a man!' But the Bible, while granting
this, never sentimentalises over it. It faces with a stern realism the
fact that there is in man an element which, if unmastered, can make
him sink lower than the beasts. It was perhaps alien to the Hebrew
way of looking at life to linger long over the question which perplexed the Greeks and drew from them such a wealth of literature—
'where does evil come from?' True, the Hebrews had in their
primitive creation stories the picture-story of the man, the woman,
the serpent and the fruit. But even this story is more concerned
with the nature of man's rebellion, and its dire consequence in the
breaking of fellowship between man and God, than with the origin
of evil. If the typical Greek question is 'Where does evil come
from?' the typical Hebrew question is 'How can evil be conquered?'
It is to this that writer after writer addresses himself, and does so
with a seriousness which shows that he has faced the strange para-
dox of man's nature—a nobility which makes him akin to the
angels, and a sinfulness which can make him create a Belsen, or
kill his wife by nagging while he is a churchwarden or mayor of the
local municipality.

Looking back over the history of the last century one can but
wish that the realism of the anthropology of the Bible had been
taken more seriously. Had that been the case, we should have heard
less of that philosophy of life which seemed to hold that, given a
little more knowledge, Utopia was round the corner. We *were*

[11] Gen. 1:31
[12] Ps. 8:5, 6 R.S.V.

given a little more knowledge—indeed, a great deal. But two world wars were round the corner, with all the horrors of atom-bombing and concentration camps. 'What a piece of work is a man!'—much depends on the tone of voice in which you quote your Shakespeare!

The Hebrew realism in regard to the nature of man needs to be taken seriously. It calls upon us to put a question mark against the gnostic view of life that the answer to man's wrongness is more knowledge—by itself. Did not T. R. Glover say somewhere that the Greeks thought that man had only to follow his nose and he would arrive at blessedness? But the Greeks had forgotten that man had a broken nose. The Hebrews never forgot it. Hence the sternness of their writings. Hence the insistence on the need of divine succour, of redemption, of a Hand stretched out to rescue us. Hence the conviction, which sounds again and again, in history, in poetry, in prophecy, in apocalyptic, that there is a moral core to the universe, a principle of judgement to be reckoned with. God may be regarded as the Father of his people—that is propounded in both Testaments. But he is also Judge. Divine love is not sentimentalism. Man, if he is to rise to the heights for which he was intended, must come to terms with this. He must exercise his moral responsibility, if he is to *live*—and life, as we shall see later, is for a Hebrew much more than physical existence.

(ii) *God.* If we go to the Bible expecting to find there a closely enunciated argument for the existence of God, we shall be disappointed. His existence is taken for granted much as the air we breathe is taken for granted. If there were no air, we should not be here. We may comment on the kind of air it is—warm, cold, blowing fiercely, breathing gently, and so on. But we do not often argue about its existence! It was something like that when the Hebrews came to think and speak—and eventually to write—about God. 'It is he that hath made us and we are his.'[13] We should not exist if he were not. But what he is *like*—that is another matter. That he cannot be depicted in stone or in art became, early in Hebrew history, a fundamental tenet of their faith. Hence the contribution of Hebrew religion to the idea of monotheism; and hence, incidentally, the poverty of the Hebrew contribution to art. 'Thou shalt not

[13] Ps. 100:3 Revised Psalter

make unto thee any graven image, or any *likeness* of any thing . . .'[14]
Hence the surprise of Titus when, during the sack of Jerusalem in
A.D. 70, on entering the Holy of Holies in the Temple he found—
nothing! No. 'No man has seen God at any time.'[15] He may not be
depicted or his image be formed. But he may be *known*. This is the
great fundamental conviction of the Hebrew prophets. If the
Greeks preached self-knowledge, the Hebrews preached that knowledge of God was everything, and man could only truly know
himself when he was at least beginning to know God. 'My people
are gone into captivity, for lack of knowledge,' laments the prophet
Isaiah.[16] When he speaks of knowledge he does not mean merely
the acquisition of intellectual facts or the equipment of mental
furniture. He means that knowledge of God which is at once the
worship of the creature directed to the Creator and the acknow-
ledgement of a relationship of the most intimate kind. Indeed the
verb to *know* used with reference to God is the identical word which
is used of physical *knowledge*, the intercourse of man and woman.
This theme is worked out in great detail by a series of Old Testament writers who depict Israel as the Bride of Yahweh and speak
of her defection from him as adultery. The nuptial element
in Hebrew religion is strong precisely because anything less
would fail to express the intimacy with which this God may be
known.

The element of the numinous is strong. The links with nature
are close. God appears to Abraham as he gazes at the stars; to Jacob
in the open during a dream; to Moses in the flaming bush. Sometimes man's reaction is sheer terror; sometimes a trembling hope;
sometimes a steady confidence. Slowly but surely, as we read the
ancient documents in roughly chronological order, we see the
emergence of a people from crude and inadequate ideas of God to
a vision of him which almost blinds us with its majesty. Slowly the
magical gives way to the ethical—the idea of naked power to the
concept of the demands of divine justice, mercy and love—till at
last, with the eighth-century prophets, we see the stern justice of

[14] Exod. 20:4
[15] John 1:18
[16] Isa. 5:13 R.V.

Amos's God, dispensing judgement to Israel's heartless neighbours and—on the principle of 'the greater the light the greater the judgement'—sterner judgement on privileged Israel herself; the infinite tenderness of Hosea's God; the kingly majesty of Isaiah's God (depicted in chapter 6 against the background of the failure of the prophet's hero-king); till at last we see a God whose rule is not confined to his chosen people but is as wide as the bounds of his world. Israel is given as a light to lighten the Gentiles. There is no limit to the vision of Deutero-Isaiah's God. He is the God of all the earth to whose worship, in the fullness of time, all men shall come. Even Cyrus is regarded as an agent in his hands, his anointed, his 'Messiah' whom he uses in the fulfilment of his purposes.

Such, in briefest outline, was the backcloth against which Jesus painted his picture of God. The metaphor of backcloth and picture, however, is wholly inadequate to convey the manner of his teaching and the content of his lessons. For he taught as much by his example and life as by his verbal formulations. As his disciples watched him at prayer, they said, 'Lord, teach us to pray'. They saw One who, to use the Old Testament language, knew God in a manner at once intimate and reverent. The contact between the One who prayed and the God to whom he prayed was patently close and real and live. Seeing that, and listening to him as he prayed, they could not argue the existence of God, as it were, at arm's length. They were in the company of One who was in the company of God. Here was the knowledge of God indeed! His teaching in a sense was extraordinarily simple—a child could begin to understand it. He said that *only* a child—or the childlike—could understand it. All of them knew what fatherhood meant—loving, personal, constant care. And all of them knew what kingship meant—authority and demand. Well, combine the two—fatherhood and kingship; combine the two—care and authority; and you will begin to see what God is like, and the nature of the human response for which he looks. A father seeks the response of love, a king the response of obedience. That is the essence of the religious life—loving obedience. That is the road to the knowledge of God. That is the path to the *summum bonum*.

'In Full Assurance of Faith'

When the early Christians looked back on the life and death of Jesus of Nazareth, and especially on the events connected with his passion, crucifixion and the immediately ensuing days, they found it hard to give expression to what they considered as having happened in what we might call the Christ-event. Some put it one way, some another. But however they put it, they were at one in the conviction that in the Person of Jesus of Nazareth there had been an irruption of goodness and power, of grace, of the mind and activity of God, for which the events of the Old Testament Scriptures were indeed a preparation but to which they could provide no adequate parallel. Here was something unique. The reign of God had broken in; the Finger of God had been at work (the phrase is used in the Old Testament only of God at work in creation, in the giving of the Law, and in the redemption of his people from slavery); the Son of God had come; the Word of God had been made flesh. Perhaps the last phrase is the most expressive of all. We owe it to the writer of the Fourth Gospel (though the thought behind the phrase had been expressed, but not in identical language, by St. Paul and by the writer of the Epistle to the Hebrews). In using the word *logos*, St. John availed himself of a term well known to Hellenic and Hebraic thinkers and writers. In this term, the two great streams of thought flowed together, though there can be little doubt that the Hebraic stream was the stronger of the two. St. John was not content to think of Jesus as one more, or even as the greatest, of the prophets. *Their* task was to be the bearers of the word of God to man. Indeed, they spoke of the word as a burden which they had to carry and deliver. But Jesus *was* the Word. He, in human flesh, *was* what God had to say to men. In his Person, the mind and heart and will of God were uniquely disclosed. Hence the voice at the baptism and again at the transfiguration—'hear *him!*' Hence the extraordinary religious phenomenon that Jews, monotheists born and bred, found themselves praying to Jesus only a very short time after the withdrawal of his body from the earthly scene. Hence the incipient trinitarianism of such a passage as this: 'Through him (i.e. Jesus) we both have access by one Spirit to the Father.'[17] Hence the daring

[17] Eph. 2:18

137

phrase of the writer of the Book of the Revelation when he refers
to the shared 'throne of God and of the Lamb'.[18] These are facets
of a phenomenon which cannot be explained in any other way than
by the conviction that in Jesus Christ, in his life and supremely in
his death and resurrection, God had broken into this world-order
in rescuing activity never so seen before.

This irruption, this invasion of grace, did not cease when Jesus
was seen no more. Many thought it would. In fact, it did not. On
the contrary, what was a localised movement soon showed itself to
be possessed of extraordinary powers of expansion. The doctrine
of the Holy Spirit, to which one would like to devote a chapter
instead of a passing paragraph, grew out of—what? The Old
Testament teaching? Yes, in part. But far more out of the experience of a group of ordinary men and women who saw the life of
Jesus continuing at work within them and who were conscious of
the outworking of his love and power in their lives. Christian
pneumatology, which occupies a much larger place in the New
Testament than many theological books deign to accord it, was no
arid doctrine neatly thought up by a synod of theologians, but was
an attempt to express, albeit in faltering language, the inexpressible
power of God at work.

(iii) *Life*. What the Bible has to say about human life emerges
from the fundamental conviction of its writers that the only worthwhile life is the holy life, that is to say, life lived according to the
mind and will of the holy God who is himself the origin of life. If
there are passages of Scripture which depict God mostly in terms
of crude power—'how *awesome* is this place; this is none other than
the house of God . . .'—the concept of power soon gives place to
the overmastering concept of the holy, thought of in terms of the
ethical. The later prophets inveigh in terrible language against any
concept of ritual, of the cult, divorced from the ethical.[19] Our
Lord's condemnation of the worst characteristics of the Pharisees
springs from a similar background of thought. St. Paul insists far
more on the harvest of the Spirit—love, joy, peace, self-control and
so on—than on the more showy gifts of glossolalia and the like. 'As

[18] Rev. 22:1
[19] Isa. 1:10 ff. is a case in point

he which hath called you is holy, so be ye holy.'[20] Only so can man live the life for which he was destined as a son of God.

'A son of God'; it is this concept which makes it impossible for the New Testament writers to believe that the dissolution of the physical body can be the end of *life*. Life as a biblical concept is more than the continuation of a heart beat. It is the continuation of a relationship entered into in the here and now and reaching its fulfilment when physical life as we know it is transcended. St. Paul struggles to express it in terms of a 'spiritual body'. St. John, in a passage marked by a delightfully frank agnosticism—'we know not what we shall be'—pin-points the essence of the thing when he says 'we shall be like him, for we shall see him as he is'.[21] That is to say, physical dissolution cannot destroy a union of love entered into here. Perhaps it is unfortunate that we have to use such words as 'endless' or 'everlasting' which to our English ears have a temporal connotation which misses the qualitative meaning of the New Testament concept. This is something more than what the Greeks meant by the immortality of the soul. This is the fulfilment and the consummation of a relationship between Redeemer and redeemed.

That the life of the redeemed in the hereafter is depicted in *corporate* imagery is not to be wondered at, for the Christian life on earth is always described in corporate terms. Those who enter into life eternal are depicted as members of a worshipping community (though there is no need of a Temple wherein to worship), as citizens of a heavenly city whose King is the Lord God. This is but the consummation of the life of the Christian here on earth. In the here and now he is a member of the *family* of God; he has come within the sphere of the *Kingdom* of God; he is a member of the *people* of God. Christian experience, while allowing full range for the exercise of individual choice and individual development, is always *corporate* experience. The doctrine of the Church is not an addendum to the main corpus of Christian doctrine, an after-thought added on to the original Gospel. It is part and parcel of the Gospel. Incorporation into Christ means incorporation into the

[20] 1 Pet. 1:15
[21] 1 John 3:2

Body of Christ, where alone is to be found the nourishment of word and sacrament.

The Church is a venerable institution. If you ask when it began, it is scarcely correct to reply 'at Pentecost'. It is older than that. Pentecost saw the renewal and the empowering of the Church. The *Christian* Church began when Jesus, walking by the Sea of Galilee, saw two pairs of brothers and called them and they followed him. But, of course, long before that there was a Church. It can be traced back to the days of Abraham, that man of faith who, at the call of God, went out though not knowing whither he went, and became the father of the faithful. Of that Church the believing and baptised Christian is a member, and if at times he is tempted to be scandalised by its failure, he checks himself by reminding himself that it is made up of sinners like himself, *simul justi et peccatores*. There is no other Body of Christ. Here the holy life of the sons of God is nourished, and given for the life of the world.

It is themes such as these which bind together the strange conglomeration of books which we call the Bible. It is such themes which give to it its unity and which constitute its relevance. For man, whether he lives two thousand years before Christ or two thousand years after him, needs to know about himself and his nature, about God and the revelation of himself which he has given to man, and about the meaning of life here and hereafter. Central to all its affirmations is the announcement of the Word made flesh. Before the imperatives of its ethics come the indicatives of God's grace. Luther was not far wrong when he called the Bible the cradle which bears Christ to us. We do not worship the cradle. We can see the variety of workmanship which has gone to the making of it. But we venerate it for the holy Burden which it bears; we approach it with the humility it deserves; and we disseminate it precisely because its story is, as we said above, *Heilsgeschichte*, salvation-story, relevant for all men of all ages, inasmuch as he who is our salvation is 'the same yesterday, today and for ever'. Scripture speaks. It moves. It influences.

Professor J. Isaacs in his essay on 'The Authorised Version and After' writes: 'A giant work, still to be done, perhaps in the old manner by committees of committees, is to trace the penetration of English religious and secular life by the substance and idiom of the English Bible. The prayers of Bishop Lancelot Andrewes and Doctor Samuel Johnson, the poetry of Shakespeare and Milton, the fiction of Bunyan, the lyrics of Blake and Hardy are but milestones on a long and fascinating journey.'[22] It is impossible to appreciate the literature of our race without an appreciation of the English Bible.

But, of course, the influence of the Bible has been far deeper than a literary influence only. Its influence on religion, on ethics, on character has been even more profound. Take, for example, the writings of St. Paul. History would seem to show that, when his message is grasped, there is a quickening of mind and conscience and a renewal of life among men. Augustine, living in an age when the old order was crashing into ruins, seized upon the truth of the Pauline gospel and wrote in such a way as to influence not only his own circle but the whole Western world in all succeeding generations. Luther laboured in his cell at the Epistle to the Galatians (which J. B. Lightfoot used to describe as the rough model of which Romans is the finished statue),[23] and the Reformation began to shake Europe. There was a transformation in his own life and thought when, 'knocking importunately at Paul . . . thirsting most ardently to know what St. Paul meant', he discovered that the Work of God is that which God works in us, the Power of God is that with which he makes us strong, the Wisdom of God is that with which he makes us wise, the Justice of God the gift with which he takes away our sin; and that faith is the means by which man abandons his own self-righteousness and apprehends the righteousness of God.[24] Colet lectures at Oxford on the Epistles of St. Paul; Erasmus feeds on the truths of the New Testament at Cambridge; and the light shines out over England. Wesley, Oxford don and

---

[22] In *Ancient and English Versions of the Bible*, p. 234
[23] J. B. Lightfoot, *St. Paul's Epistle to the Galatians* (Macmillan, 1865), p. 48
[24] See Gordon Rupp, *The Righteousness of God* (Hodder and Stoughton, 1953), esp. p. 121 ff. Luther wrote of the Epistle to the Galatians that 'it is my epistle; I have betrothed myself to it: it is my wife' (quoted in J. B. Lightfoot, op. cit., p. 66)

returned missionary, meets with a little group of godly men studying Luther's commentary on the Epistle to the Galatians, and finds
his heart 'strangely warmed'. That 'warmth' moved him to travel
on horseback up and down England, into his extreme old age; and
who can say how large a part that mission played in averting from
England the kind of revolution which had recently drenched
France in blood?[25] Dr. A. W. F. Blunt was right when he wrote of
St. Paul's insight into the innermost truth of Christian experience,
'The Church has often failed to realise Paul's doctrine in its
practical application. But, whenever Christianity has been at its
best, it has always been a Christianity which found in Pauline
doctrine the real illumination of that which it believed.'[26]

We have referred to intellectual and religious giants of days gone
by—Augustine, Luther, Colet, Erasmus, Wesley. We could mention names in our own day—a Karl Barth on the Continent, a
William Temple in England (his chief inspiration was St. John),[27]
a Niebuhr in America—all men whose minds and souls have been
stirred by the message of the Bible. But the same might be said of
men of affairs. One example may be given. W. K. Hancock tells
how Jan Smuts discovered in St. Paul, during his student days at
Cambridge, in his treatise on Law, 'a fundamental canon of human
development; sixty years later, it was to St. Paul, not to Plato, that
he returned when he felt the need to strengthen the foundations of
his faith during the war against Hitler'.[28]

There is another phenomenon which calls for mention. It is this:
the Bible speaks, not only to the intellectually powerful, but also to
the unlettered and the simple. Perhaps this is not wholly to be
wondered at, for St. Paul remarked, in writing to the Corinthians,
that 'few of you are men of wisdom, by any human standard; few

[25] cp. Richard Church writing of John Wesley: 'this man . . . forestalled
the excesses of the French Revolution from setting fire to the English
social structure . . .' (*The Wonder of Words*, Hutchinson, 1970, p. 15)
[26] A. W. F. Blunt, *The Epistle of Paul to the Galatians* (Oxford University Press, 1925), p. 30
[27] *Readings in St. John's Gospel*, p. v. 'For as long as I can remember I
have had more love for St. John's Gospel than for any other book . . . with
St. John I am at home'
[28] W. K. Hancock, *Smuts* (Cambridge University Press, 1962), vol. 1,
p. 38

are powerful or highly born'.[29] The writer of the Acts of the Apostles says that their opponents noticed that the early Christians at Jerusalem were 'unlearned and ignorant men'.[30] And Celsus, one of the opponents of the Christian movement in the second century, mocked at the lowly social status of many of the adherents of Christianity in his day. Certain it is that those who are most experienced in the exercise of ordinary pastoral duties among all kinds of people find that there is about the Bible a kind of *universal* appeal. There may, for example, be many problems to the scholar about the precise meaning—even about the precise translation—of the opening verses of the fourteenth chapter of the Gospel according to St. John. But anyone whose task it is to minister to sorrowing or fearful people will tell you that verses such as these have brought comfort and strength to men and women of all kinds of social and educational background. The first chapter of St. John is one of the profoundest documents ever penned; but again and again it has proved a source of nourishment and inspiration to the simple. The fifty-third chapter of Isaiah is to the scholar a passage full of difficulties of interpretation—almost every sentence is patient of more than one translation. But again and again it has lit up for the simple-hearted the meaning of the Passion of Jesus and something of its significance in the salvation of the world.

Nor is this the case in English-speaking countries only. Anyone who moved, as the writer did for a short while in 1955, among those in Kenya who had withstood the terrors of Mau Mau persecution, will know to what a tremendous extent those unlettered Christians drew their strength from the wells of Scripture. We may explain it as we will, but the fact remains that for scholar and ignoramus, for Eastern and Western, for black and white, the Bible has a message which is always fresh and alive. Einstein bore his witness to the fact that when all other movements, universities included, bowed the knee to Hitler, it was the Christian Church which stood up to him. It is to be noted that the Church which opposed Hitler and did so much to break his power was a Church deeply indebted to and nourished on the word of God. Particularly

[29] 1 Cor. 1:26 N.E.B.
[30] Acts 4:13

in times of stress and strain, the Scriptures speak their message in a way almost unbelievably relevant to a particular situation. The Psalms, for example, from one point of view are ancient national poems, marred, in parts, by a vengeful spirit which the Christian mind rejects in any literal sense. They were written out of national agony and personal stress centuries before the Christian era dawned. They reflect the persecution and perplexities of a pre-Christian age. But the voice of the experience of the Church is unanimous in averring that, in times of stress, national and personal, these Psalms have a way of rising above their original local application, of 'speaking to our condition', of forming the prayer of Christians who, with fuller knowledge, worship the same God as did the writers of the Psalms many centuries ago. The Scriptures have a way of being the material on which the Holy Spirit of God breathes, and from which he brings forth light and truth to the Christian conscience.

In the novel by the Nobel Prize-winner, Alexander Solzhenitsyn, *The First Circle*, there is a description of an old university professor, Dmitri Dmitrich Govyainov-Shakhovskoy. He was what is called 'a character'. 'It was terrible trying to take down his lectures . . . It was impossible to grasp his ideas at the time, but whenever Nerzhin and one of his comrades shared the work of taking notes and managed afterwards to reconstruct what he had said, they were moved as one is moved by the shimmering light of distant stars.'[31]

It has been so—and is so—with the biblical writings. The style, for example, of St. Paul is often complex—the fact that he dictated his letters did not make matters easier. His thought is involved. His Rabbinic allusions are sometimes difficult for a Gentile to follow. His views of certain non-essentials—women's apparel is a case in point—are typically first century. But those who have read him, pondered him, and soaked themselves in his great concepts down the years, have found themselves 'moved as one is moved by the shimmering light of distant stars'. What is true of St. Paul's writings is true, in the main, of Scripture as a whole. In its work of translation, dissemination, explication, the Church may proceed

[31] Alexander Solzhenitsyn, *The First Circle* (Collins and Harvill, 1968), p. 46

'in full assurance of faith', with a deep humility and at the same
time with a God-given confidence.

As the Second World War was grinding to a halt, John Masefield
wrote words which apply to the Church in its mission of communication:

> After destruction, lo, a human need,
> For folly, knowledge, and for blindness, sight.
> Our harvests, who shall reckon? *We sow seed*
> *That unborn generations may have light.*

Epilogue

F. R. Barry, sometime Bishop of Southwell, tells in his auto-biography[1] how, when he went on a visit to Australia in the early 1930s, 'a British passport was like a magic carpet and it was not yet a liability either to be white or to be an Englishman. Twenty-five years later we made the same voyage, and found that we had to obtain a special visa to go ashore at Port Said. *Civis Britannicus sum* meant almost nothing.' The walls are going up—walls of division which separate nation from nation and man from man. The proliferation of passports is but a symbol of the barriers which multiply and which alienate us one from another. In many nations today, missionaries from the West are excluded (Communist China is the example *par excellence*), or, if not excluded, are allowed to continue their work only on sufferance or under strictly limiting conditions. It calls for no great prophetic insight to forecast that, with the renewed vitality of some of the ancient eastern religions and with the upsurge of nationalistic aspirations, doors now open to missionary personnel will before long be closed.

What do these facts mean for twentieth-century Christian strategy? They mean, as our missionary statesmen have long ago seen clearly, that only those with high qualifications and specialised skills will be likely to find a welcome in the so-called emerging nations. But they also mean that, if the Christian message is to penetrate the walls which are going up around us, the Christian Church must give its attention, *in a way it has not done up to now*, to the use of the mass media, to the printed word, to drama, to radio, to television.

Books can often go where persons cannot. Christopher Morley has reminded us, 'When you sell a man a book, you do not sell him

[1] F. R. Barry, *Period of My Life* (Hodder and Stoughton, 1970), p. 119–20

146

just twelve ounces of paper, ink and glue; you sell him a whole new life.' This is the thesis of the preceding chapters, supremely true if that book be the Bible, and true—so history has shown again and again—of those books which expound the principles of life to which the Bible bears its constant witness. If this be fact, then the work of the Bible Societies must cease to be (as it still is, in the estimation of some respectable church people) the concern of a devout minority who 'have a thing about the Bible'. The work of those Societies must be recognised for what in fact it is, of the very *esse* of the life and work of the Church. All down the centuries, the Church has gone to the world with the Bible in its hand, translated in the languages of the nations which it has sought to evangelise in its response to its Master's command. That book is its indispensable tool. History would seem to indicate that where a biblically-based Christianity has not penetrated deeply into society, there the Church has shrivelled and died—North Africa, once a chain of thriving Christian provinces, then within a century almost completely overrun by Muslim forces, is a case in point. 'As the Punic language never embraced the Bible . . . the Christianising process was not permanent.'[2]

Bishop Charles Gore once said, 'There is no surer way of getting men and women of whatever religious tradition again into the presence of Jesus of Nazareth than by giving them the Gospels in their own tongue.' The long story of the Christian Church underlines the truth of the Bishop's words, and pinpoints the priority of biblical translation, illustration, annotation, dissemination, on an ecumenical basis and on a scale hitherto unreached.

But the translation and dissemination of the Bible is only the beginning, though it is the *sine qua non*, of the Church's work in this field. The divine command to 'feed my sheep' includes the feeding of their minds. The best antidote to the mass of filth which pours from some of the presses is the production of an even greater mass of good material. A revival of Christian concern for the arts is greatly to be desired. We need men of the calibre of T. S. Eliot, C. S. Lewis, Christopher Fry, George Bell, in their various ways

---

[2] A. Harnack, *The Mission and Expansion of Christianity* (Williams and Norgate, 1908), vol. II, p. 297

to help us to penetrate the structures of literature, art, theatre, and mass media with Christian æsthetic insights—all too rarely do we speak meaningfully to the people of our generation through the arts.

We need to capture the imagination of the best graduates of our universities with the possibility of feeding the minds of millions with the message of Christ and of bringing them captive to his service which is perfect freedom. In a remarkable way, agencies of compassion such as Oxfam, War on Want, Shelter, have made their appeal to the ideals of the young. God be praised! Now it is the task of the Church, I would say its supreme task, to help them to see that a man rescued from physical want but bereft of an adequate philosophy of life is a pauper indeed. When we have met the material needs of a nation, we have only made a beginning. 'It was hard to face a country marred by physical ruin; it was far harder to rule a people steeped in ignorance, unaware of books.'[3] So Eleanor Duckett wrote of King Alfred's England. It is still abundantly true of any nation.

Cardinal Suenens, that man of vision, has told us that our great need is 'a theology of the actual, which is nothing more than a Christian gaze upon what is happening at the moment and its interpretation'.[4] Such a gaze will reveal a world of men with hungry minds, minds which can only be fully fed with the truth as it is in Jesus. It will also reveal the need for an army of men and women, mostly young, who will give themselves, their gifts, their insights, their skills, their love to the feeding of those minds. There can be no greater life-work.

[3] Eleanor Duckett, *Alfred the Great and his England* (Collins, 1957), p. 98

[4] L. J. Suenens, *Co-responsibility in the Church* (Burns and Oates/ Herder, 1968), p. 210

Member Societies and Associate Members of the United Bible Societies

MEMBER SOCIETIES

American Bible Society
Argentine Bible Society
Austrian Bible Society
Belgian Bible Society
Bible Society of Brazil
Bible Society of Burma
Bible Society of India
Bible Society of Singapore,
   Malaysia and Brunei
Bible Society of Mexico
Bible Society in New Zealand
Bible Society of South Africa
British and Foreign Bible Society
B.F.B.S. in Australia
Canadian Bible Society
Ceylon Bible Society
Danish Bible Society
Finnish Bible Society
French Bible Society
Germany (BRD)
Germany (DDR)
Hibernian Bible Society
Icelandic Bible Society
Indonesian Bible Society
Japan Bible Society
Korean Bible Society
National Bible Society of Scot-
   land
Netherlands Bible Society
Norwegian Bible Society
Philippine Bible Society
Swedish Bible Society
Swiss Bible Society
West Pakistan Bible Society

ASSOCIATE MEMBERS

Bible Society: Cameroun Gabon
Bible Society in Chile
Bible Society in Colombia
Bible Society of Congo
East Pakistan Bible Society
Bible Society of Ethiopia
Bible Society in Malawi
Bible Society of Nigeria
Bible Society in Peru
Bible Society in Portugal
Bible Society in Taiwan
Bible Society in Venezuela

Bible Society of Ghana	Bible Society in Vietnam
Bible Society in Hong Kong	Bible Society in Zambia
Bible Society in Italy	Malagasy Bible Society

APPENDIX II

'A Solemn and Urgent Appeal'

In September 1965 there was held in Teheran a World Congress of Ministers of Education on the Eradication of Illiteracy. The Congress, 'convinced that the struggle against illiteracy, aimed at the total eradication from our planet of the scourge of ignorance, is a moral imperative for our generation', concluded its recommendations with:

A SOLEMN AND URGENT APPEAL

To the United Nations, its Specialised Agencies and, in the first place to UNESCO;
to regional bodies concerned with development in general and education in particular;
to non-governmental organisations which include assistance, direct or indirect, to education in their operational programmes;
to religious, social and cultural institutions;
to national and international foundations, both public and private;
to educators, scientists and scholars, to economic and trade union leaders, and to all men of goodwill:
to do everything in their power to arouse public opinion with a view to intensifying and accelerating the world-wide attack on illiteracy; and in particular to exert their influence on all responsible leaders:

(*a*) to ensure that literacy work is an integral and essential part of every development plan in countries where illiteracy is rife;

(*b*) to increase, so far as may be practicable and appropriate, the national and international resources set aside for the fight against illiteracy;

(*c*) to make possible the provision of additional resources for development in general and for literacy work in particular as and when further funds become available through a reduction of military expenditures or for other reasons;

(*d*) to harness to the full all available information media for propagating the new concept of adult literacy;

(*e*) to ensure that priority in the allocation of available resources is accorded to the fight against the great human afflictions that constitute a major threat to peace, namely hunger, disease and ignorance, among which illiteracy occupies a place of key importance.[1]

[1]Quoted in Charles Jeffries: *Illiteracy: A World Problem*, pp. 169-70

Index to Biblical References

OLD TESTAMENT

Genesis
1:31 133
3:7 60
24:60 50

Exodus
3:5 14
3:14 14
20:4 135

Leviticus
21:5 50

Numbers
23:8 50

2 Samuel
1:20 78

Job
3:3 73

Psalms
8:5 ff. 133
23 62
63:4 65
91:5 58
100:3 134
103:13 14
137:9 131

Proverbs
3:17 65

Song of Solomon
2:12 65, 68

Isaiah
1:10 ff. 138
5:13 135
6 136
44:28 14
45:1 14
49:15 15, 131
53 143

Jeremiah
8:22 58
23:29 76
43:10 14

APOCRYPHA

1 Maccabees
4:46 17

NEW TESTAMENT

Matthew
1:1–17 16

Luke
3:1 16
3:22 21
4:1, 14, 18 21
15:13 71
17:27 67
19:10 65

John
1 143
1:18 135
10:10 17
14:1 ff. 143
14:26 23
20:31 27

Index to Biblical References

Acts
2:41–47 22
4:13 143
8:1, 4 31

Romans
8:14 21
12:2 21

I Corinthians
1:26 143
2:1 19
8:5 17, 100
9:14 20
11:26 19

Galatians
4:4 16
5:19–23, 25 21
6:10 24

Ephesians
1:1 28
2:18 137
4:5 20
5:14 27

Colossians
4:16 28

Philemon
22 131

I Timothy
3:16 27

2 Timothy
2:9 93
4 52
4:13 131

Hebrews
1:1 14
10:22 129

James
2:3 67
3:5, 6 67
5:11 15

I Peter
1:15 139
2:9 13

I John
3:1 65
3:2 139

Revelation
22:1 138

General Index

Abbott, Walter M., 94, 95, 98
Abraham, 16
Adelphius, 35
Aelfric, 39
Aldhelm, 38
Aldred, 39
Alfred, King, 38, 148
American Bible Society, 85, 86, 88, 106
Andrewes, Lancelot, 63, 64, 65, 141
Apocrypha, 74
Arles, Council of, 35
Arundel, Archbishop, 44, 93
Augustine, 34, 141, 142
Authorised Version, 62–65, 67, 68, 69, 72, 75, 77

Bacon, Francis, 65
Baptist Missionary Society, 82
Barry, F. R., 146
Barth, Karl, 142
Bea, Cardinal A., 95, 96
Bede, The Venerable, 37, 38, 39
Béguin, Olivier, 89, 93
Bell, G. K. A., 37, 88, 92, 147
Berggrav, E. J., 88, 89, 91–93
Beza, 61
Bible for Today, The, 104
Bible Reading Fellowship, 107–8
Bible Society of France, 88
Bickersteth, Edward, 124
Bishops' Bible, 61
Blake, William, 141
Blunt, A. W. F., 142
Board for Social Responsibility, 116, 120

Book of Common Prayer, 57, 72
Borlaug, N. E., 114
Boys, John, 64
Bratcher, R. G., 79
Breeches Bible, 60
British and Foreign Bible Society, 82–89, 101, 102, 123, 124, 126
Brown, Lester R., 113–14
Bruce, F. F., 74, 75
Bunyan, John, 48, 141
Burkitt, F. C., 9
Busia, Dr. K. A., 111
Butterworth, C. C., 41, 55, 58

Caedmon, 37, 38
Calvin, 61, 81
Canton, William, 83
Carey, William, 82
Carrington, Archbishop P., 28
Caxton, William, 43
Celsus, 143
Chadwick, Owen, 72, 120, 130
Charles, Thomas, 84
Children's Special Service Mission, 108
Chirgwin, A. M., 125
Christian Communication Centre, 127
Christian Literature Council of C.B.M.S., 126
Chrysostom, 36
Church Missionary Society, 82
Church, Richard, 142
Cohen, J. M., 75
Colet, John, 49, 53, 54, 141, 142
Columbus, Christopher, 81

Complutensian Polyglot, 60
Constance, Council of, 45
Coptic Version, 32
Coverdale, Miles, 53–58, 59, 60, 61, 62, 65, 66, 67
Craigie, William A., 34
Cranmer, Thomas, 56, 59
Cromwell, Thomas, 53, 56, 60
Cuthbert, St., 39
Cyrus, 14

Daiches, David, 55
Damasus, Pope, 33
Darby, J. N., 72
Darlow, T. H., 80
Davey, Noel, 129
David, 14, 16
Davison, Leslie, 19, 81
Dead Sea Scrolls, 76
Dillistone, F. W., 16, 35
Dodd, C. H., 20, 26, 78
Douai Old Testament, 62
Driver, Godfrey, 69, 78
Driver, S. R., 68
Duckett, Eleanor, 148
Duff, Alexander, 10

Eborius, 35
Ecumenical Movement, 84–86
Edinburgh Conference 1910, 85
Edward VI, 53
Einstein, Albert, 143
Eliot, T. S., 37, 58, 63, 147
Erasmus, D., 49, 50, 53, 54, 57, 65, 141, 142
Ethiopic Version, 32

Farrar, F. W., 54
Feed the Minds, 126–8
Fisher, H. A. L., 43
Fleming, Richard, 45
Forshall, Josiah, 41, 46

Foxe, John, 49
Fry, Christopher, 37, 147
Fuller, Thomas, 45

Geneva Bible, 60, 61, 62
Gideons, 106
Glover, T. R., 21, 134
God's Word for a New Age, 124
Goethe, 19
Good News for Modern Man, 79
Goodspeed, Edgar, 73
Gore, Charles, 147
Göring, Herman, 91
Great Bible, 60
Greenslade, S. L., 47, 53
Grocyn, William, 54

Halifax, Lord, 91
Hall, Edward, 51
Hampton Court Conference, 63
Hancock, W. K., 142
Hardy, Thomas, 141
Harnack, A., 147
Harris, J. Rendel, 26
Harvey, A. E., 103
Hassall, Christopher, 37
Henn, T. R., 65
Henry VIII, 56
Herbert, A. S., 80
Hereford, Nicholas, 41–2, 44, 45, 47, 65
Herodotus, 69
Hilda, St., of Whitby, 37
Hilder, Rowland, 104
Himmler, 91
Hoare, H. W., 42, 48, 56, 58
Hodges, J. P., 57
Hogg, W. R., 81
Holbein, Hans, 56, 60
Hooker, Richard, 63, 65
Hort, F. J. A., 68, 69, 71
Hoskyns, Edwyn, 129
Hughes, Joseph, 124

Hugo de Sancto Caro, 61
Humanae Vitae, 115
Humphreys, A. R., 77
Hunt, Geoffrey, 75, 78
Hunter, A. M., 28
Huxley, Julian, 115

Ignatius, 33
Illiteracy, 116–19
International Bible Reading Association, 108
International Catholic Federation, 96
Isaacs, J., 49, 59, 140

James I, 63
Jasper, Ronald C. D., 37
Jay, Eric, 115
Jeffries, Charles, 116, 117, 118
Jerome, 24, 33, 34, 55, 93
Jerusalem Conference, 1928, 85
Johnson, Alex, 91
Johnson, President L., 122
Johnson, Pamela Hansford, 122
Johnson, Samuel, 141
Joint Action for Christian Literature Overseas, 126
Juda, Leo, 56
Judas Maccabaeus, 17

Keating, Charles, 121
Kenyon, F. G., 38, 56
King James Version (*see* Authorised Version)
Kinnaird, Lady, 85
Kirkegaard, S., 13
Knighton, Henry, 46
Knox, John, 61
Knox, Ronald, 74, 76

Langton, Archbishop S., 61
Latin Bible, 32

Laubach, Frank, 119
League of Nations, 84
Lechler, G., 41
Lehtonen, Archbishop A., 88
Lenin, 117
Léon-Dufour, Xavier, 25
Lewis, C. S., 58, 74
Lightfoot, J. B., 69, 141
Lilje, Hans, 88
Linacre, Thomas, 54
Lindisfarne Gospels, 39
Living Bible, 79
Living New Testament, 79
Lomax, D. W., 127
London Missionary Society, 82
Lumby, J. R., 46
Luther, Martin, 49, 50, 81, 141, 142

Macaulay, Lord, 63, 75
Macaulay, Zachary, 124
Mace, Daniel, 67
Madden, Frederic, 41, 46
Madras Conference, 1938, 85
Malthus, Thomas, 113
Mannering, L. G., 107
Manning, Bernard Lord, 21
Manson, T. W., 13
Mao, Chairman, 119
Marlowe, Christopher, 65
Martin, Pope, 45
Mary Tudor, 53, 60, 61
Masefield, John, 145
Matthew Bible, 59–60, 61
McHardy, W. D., 78
Metzger, B. M., 34
Mexico Conference, 1961, 85
Milligan, G., 70
Milton, John, 16, 48, 141
Modern Reader's Bible, 72
Moffatt, James, 72–73, 76
Moltke, von, 91
More, Thomas, 51, 53, 54
Morley, Christopher, 146

Moses, 14
Mott, John R., 85, 86, 91
Moule, H. F., 80
Moulton, R. G., 72
Mozley, J. F., 49, 52, 53, 59

Napoleon, 82
National Bible Society of Scotland,
  86, 88, 126
Nebuchadnezzar, 14
Nero, 23
Netherlands Bible Society, 86–87,
  88
Netter, Thomas, 45
New Delhi Conference, 1961, 85,
  124
New English Bible, 67, 68, 75–79
Nicolson, James, 56, 62
Niebuhr, R., 142
Niemöller, Martin, 92
Nixon, President R., 121, 122
Norwegian Bible Society, 88,
  92

Oldham, J. H., 85
Overall, John, 64, 65
Ovid, 132
Oxfam, 126, 148

Paddock, Paul, 113
Paddock, William, 113
Parker, Archbishop Matthew, 61
Paton, William, 9
Paul, Pope, 95
Pavlova, 19
Peake, A. S., 34
Péguy, C. P., 14
Peshitta Version, 33
Phillips, J. B., 74–75, 104
Plato, 99, 132, 142
Pliny, the Elder, 16

Pope, Gregory XVI, 94; Leo IX,
  94; Pius VII, 93; Pius VIII, 94;
  Pius IX, 94
Population Explosion, 113–16
Pornography, 120–3
Psalter, Coverdale, 57–58
Ptolemy, Philadelphus, 17
Purver, Anthony, 68
Purvey, John, 42, 43–44, 47, 65
Purvis, J. S., 37
Pusey, E. B., 130

Quem Quaerites, 36
Quiller-Couch, Arthur, 45
Quisling, 91

Ramsey, Archbishop A. M., 130
Reid, J. K. S., 78
Religious Tract Society, 83, 124
Response, 109
Restitutus, 35
Reuchlin, J., 55
Revised Standard Version, 73–74
Revised Version, 67, 68
Reynolds, John, 64, 65
Rheims New Testament, 62
Richmond, Legh, 124
Rieu, C. H., 75
Rieu, E. V., 75
Robarts, Miss, 85
Robertson, E. H., 72, 125
Robinson, H. Wheeler, 35, 49
Roe, James M., 83, 89
Rogers, John, 59, 65
Royal Injunction, 56
Rupp, Gordon, 141

Salvation Army, 109
Sawtrey, William, 44
Sayers, Dorothy, 13, 37
Scripture Union, 108

Seebohm, F., 54
Seeley, John, 120
Selwyn, E. G., 28
Septuagint, 17–19, 29
Shaftesbury, Lord, 120
Shakespeare, William, 65, 132, 141
Shelley, P. B., 65
Shelter, 148
Smalley, B., 48
Smith, J. M. Powis, 73
Smith, Miles, 64
Smuts, Jan, 142
Society for Promoting Christian Knowledge, 83, 109, 123
Society for the Propagation of the Gospel in Foreign Parts, 83
Söderblom, Archbishop N., 92
Solomon, 14
Soldier's Armour, The, 108–109
Solzhenitsyn, Alexander, 144
Speaight, Robert, 36
Spenser, Edmund, 65
Spurgeon, C. H., 108
Stephens, Robert, 61
Stirling, John, 104
Streeter, B. H., 25
Student Christian Movement, 85
Suenens, Cardinal L. J., 148
Swift, Charles, 102
Sykes, Margery, 107
Sylvester, Nigel, 108
Syriac Bible, 32

Tiberius, 15
Titus, 135
Today's English Version, 79, 104, 105
Trevelyan, G. M., 36, 40, 41, 52, 83
Tunstall, Cuthbert, 51
Tyndale, William, 47–53, 54, 55, 56, 57, 58
Tyrrell, Graeme, 88

UNESCO, 117, 118
United Bible Societies, 79, 84 88–98, 101, 103, 125, 126 *See* Appendix I for list of National Bible Societies
United Nations Organisation, 84
United Society for Christian Literature, 124, 126
United Society for the Propagation of the Gospel, 124
Universities Mission to Central Africa, 124
University Presses of Oxford and Cambridge, 78
Uppsala Conference, 1968, 85

Vallotton, Annie, 79, 104, 106
Vatican II Documents, 94, 95
Vaughan, Robert, 43
Vulgate, 33, 74

Taylor, G. Rattray, 116
Taverner Bible, 60
Temple, John R., 89
Temple, Archbishop William, 27, 85, 142
Tennyson, Alfred Lord, 46
Thomson, Ian, 108
't Hooft, W. A. Visser, 88, 89, 92, 118

Walter, N. Hardy, 50
Warham, Archbishop William, 51
War on Want, 148
Waters, Charles, 108
Waugh, Evelyn, 74
Weerasinghe, S. J. de S., 125
Wegener, G. S., 131
Weigle, L. A., 72
Wesley, John, 141, 142

Westcott, B. F., 49, 55, 68, 69, 71
Weymouth, R. F., 72
Wilder, Robert P., 86
Wilkie, Wendell, 100
Wilkinson, A. H., 57
Willebrands, Cardinal J., 95, 97
Willey, Basil, 77, 78
William of Malmesbury, 38
Williams, A. Lukyn, 26
Williams, C. H., 48
Williams, Charles, 37
Williams, George, 85
Wilson, R. Mercer, 47
Wolfensberger, G. H., 125
Wolsey, Cardinal Thomas, 51
Wordsworth, 43

Workman, H. B., 41, 44
World Council of Churches, 112, 126
World Health Organisation, 84
Wycliffe, John, 41–47, 49, 53, 54, 60, 62, 65, 67, 93
Wright, W. Aldis, 49

Young Men's Christian Association, 85
Young Women's Christian Association, 85

Zwingli, Ulrich, 56